Trees
of Life

MAX ADAMS

Princeton University Press

Princeton and Oxford

PREVIOUS PAGE

The Dark Hedges, an avenue of beech trees
in Ballymoney, Northern Ireland

Published in the United States and Canada in 2021
by Princeton University Press
41 William Street
Princeton, New Jersey 08540
press.princeton.edu

First published in the UK in 2019 by Head of Zeus Ltd

10 9 8 7 6 5 4 3 2 1

Library of Congress Control Number 2020942988
Hardcover ISBN 978-0-691-21273-9
Ebook ISBN 978-0-691-21861-8

Designed by Heather Bowen

Printed and bound in Slovenia

Contents

Introduction

OPPOSITE

Camille Pissarro, *Le Verger* (The Orchard)
1872.

What is a tree of life? What makes a tree useful? The short answer is that all trees are life-giving; all are useful. Trees, like the oceans, drive the earth's climate and its incomparable biodiversity, absorbing carbon dioxide, pollutants and the energy of sunlight and giving out oxygen. Trees cycle water and gaseous nitrogen, act as air conditioners and provide habitats for millions of species of other plants, insects, birds, mammals and amphibians. They stabilize and enrich soils, slow down floods.

A single veteran tree standing in a field may host more than 300 species of birds and insects. Exploiting it for food, they also use it as a place to nest and reproduce, take refuge from predators in the cracks and fissures of its bark, or as a perch from which to advertise their wares to potential mates. Trees forming a continuous canopy – as woods or forests – create biomes on a grander scale, sometimes spanning nations and continents as a huge living organism of almost infinite interlocking and interdependent biological and behavioural relationships. When trees die their materials are recycled or act as carbon sinks.

For early humans, an intelligent species foraging in the savannah forests of East Africa and highly dependent on trees, they have been partners in a great cultural adventure. Trees provide shelter and shade as well as materials for constructing the most elemental and elegant tools and building shelters. We eat their fruit, use their leaves, bark and roots for medicines; their wood fuelled the fires that liberated us as a thinking, creative species. Trees have colonized every continent that supports permanent human communities; they, like us, are adaptable and resourceful. At least 60,000 species have evolved during the last 300 million years, brilliantly responding to every opportunity and threat that nature offers.

Trees' beauty, adaptability and resilience, their longevity and apparent stoicism have also inspired humans. The role of trees in connecting the heavens and the earth, life and death in ever-renewing cycles can seem almost magical. Mythology makes much of their supposed wisdom, their supernatural abilities and their propensity to host living spirits. Artists and writers have eulogized,

anthropomorphized, satirized and observed trees over millennia. As botanists and biologists study the miraculous workings of trees they seem to become more, not less, marvellous and complex. We know that trees can communicate with each other above and below ground; that they can draw up water from the soil to improbable heights; that they effortlessly and routinely create solid matter from light, gas and water; that they have found all manner of means to reproduce at a distance with immovable potential partners.

Humans are restless, curious, empirical experimenters with nature. From the first use of a sharp tool to split a log or peel bark, communities have explored and exploited trees over the best part of a million years. In every habitable region of the planet intimate practical knowledge of their uses, materials, propagation and behaviour has been accumulated and passed on to new generations. In the Caribbean young children and visitors are warned not to shelter from rain beneath the poisonous manchineel tree (*Hippomane mancinella*) for fear of horrible blisters, and never to eat its promising-looking fruit. The herders of the Altai mountains in Kazakhstan long since learned to trust their pigs and horses to find the sweetest varieties of wild apples. In Southeast Asia the knowledge that certain trees, when damaged, exude a mouldable and waterproof milky-white substance was acquired thousands of years ago. The memory of the genius who first dried and roasted the bean of the cacao tree of the Andes to taste the food of the gods is lost in the mists of time.

In this book I celebrate the richness of our relationship with trees, woods and forests in a series of portraits of those trees that have spawned particularly interesting relations with human communities. In many cases these are stories of deep local knowledge followed by global discovery, exploitation, environmental fallout and social oppression. In others, obscure and unprepossessing trees have turned out to hold potential solutions to the challenges of modern life through their medicinal properties or their status as keystones in subsistence strategies for some of the world's poorest communities. Where possible, I have illustrated the stories with fine photography or with paintings by great artists or botanical illustrators.

Individual species have, quite naturally, found themselves fitting into a number of themes. In the first chapter I look at those trees that have yielded materials of great practical value – from timber with a huge range of handy characteristics to bark for paper and rope, nuts for lighting and seed cases for percussion instruments. I devote a chapter to the edible fruits and nuts, some better known than others; another to trees that have given us special culinary ingredients and traditions. Dyes, essences and medicines are the focus of a dozen or so tree profiles, while a whole section is devoted to what I call trees for the planet – species so valuable to all humanity that they must be protected from loss by neglect or ignorance. I have also chosen a select few species for a chapter called 'Supertrees' – a baker's dozen of arboreal A-listers that punch far above their weight. Some trees might have sat comfortably in other chapters but I hope that, as a whole, my choices – a very small selection out of thousands of 'useful' species – will encourage readers to learn more about these givers of life on which we rely so much and about the communities who value and protect these natural riches under our care.

In a world of plastics, concrete, steel, creeping deserts and dwindling mineral resources, it is worth reminding ourselves of these ever-giving biological, chemical and engineering marvels that can and will sustain so many of our material and aesthetic needs, if only we allow them space, and time.

CHAPTER 1

Cork, Rubber, Mulberry:
a cornucopia

THERE IS NOTHING QUITE LIKE WOOD FOR UTILITY, adaptability and beauty. The earliest hunter-gatherers must have discovered nearly all the things you can do with a stick, from foraging for ants in a termite mound to making a sprung trap to catch a rabbit. Aboriginal peoples of Australia learned to start a fire with sticks from the Austral mulberry (*Hedycarya angustifolia*) thousands of years ago. Bigger sticks might ward off predators or make an improvised fence; once sharpened or weighted they might be used for attack or defence. Wood in the round, in all its varieties – from ultra-dense to super-light – tends to be strong in compression and tension, and woodsmen all over the world have identified and used wood from the best trees in their neighbourhood for all sorts of material applications: from the walls and roofs of their houses to constructing causeways across bogs.

Cut across the natural grain of a tree trunk or branch and a new world is opened to the curious artisan: wood splits along its grain and can be turned into boards, planks, wedges, furniture and parts for any number of devices. Some trees, like the super-heavy lignum vitae (*Guaiacum officinale*) produce timber that has proved better than any modern alternative for some heavy-engineering applications. And wood as a sustainable construction material is once again being taken very seriously by architects.

Trees don't just provide wood: the cork oak is famous for its uniquely spongy bark, which can be harvested regularly; and many trees have bark that produces long, stringy fibres used for making rope, matting, fishing nets, even clothes and paper. The bark of a North American birch was used by fishermen and trappers to make strong, flexible, lightweight canoes.

In this first chapter, species from four continents illustrate the range of materials harvested from trees by local communities who historically used them as DIY stores for roofing, building, insulating and padding materials. Silkworms and farm animals fed on their leaves, their husks made good containers and oil from their seeds was used in cooking and lighting. One of the traditional principles of the woodsman is to utilize every part of a tree: whatever can't be

ABOVE
Four members of the Kayan people collect gutta percha from a tree trunk, Sarawak, northwestern Borneo.

OPPOSITE
A turner or bodger working in West Wycombe, Buckinghamshire, c.1945. Chair legs were traditionally turned or 'bodged' on a foot-driven pole lathe.

used to make or concoct necessary objects is burned as fuel. Some trees are valued as special individuals; others are planted or nurtured as crops, to be cut every few years. Many trees can be harvested repeatedly without harm while some must be replanted to ensure the next generation. But none can be treated as if they do not belong to a wider ecosystem: trees can be replaced but ancient woods and forests cannot.

Tied up with the special physical properties of each tree is a huge wealth of knowledge – empirical, historical and mythical. Some trees are regarded as so fundamental to the stories and identities of the places where they grow, that they appear as national emblems on flags or postage stamps. Many, many more trees than can be included here are just as important to their communities as the familiar hazel was to European farmers and herders for thousands of years. Some are now more or less neglected in favour of mass-produced, identical factory products – and it is ironic that plastic and oil fuels, those scourges of modern environmental sensitivities, are derived from the fossilized remains of trees that died many millions of years ago.

It is inescapably the case that, in researching the histories of many of the trees in this book, some uncomfortable historical realities have come to light. In particular, the exploitive activities of colonizers, slave owners and entrepreneurial industrialists from the great European powers have left enduring economic, social and environmental legacies – with both broad humanitarian benefits and more negative consequences in equal measure. The view that these trees provide of history as a story of creativity and discovery must be balanced with a woeful record of oppression and exploitation. The trees in this chapter are witnesses to both.

Isonandra Gutta Hook.
Tubanbaum.

Gutta-percha
Palaquium gutta

LOCAL NAMES: TABAN; GETAH PERCA (MALAY)

The chances are that, if you have ever undergone root-canal treatment at the dentist, the hole was filed with a stick of the natural latex called gutta-percha. And if you happen to be a student of the history of telegraphy you will know that the first transatlantic wireless cables, laid in the middle of the nineteenth century, were sheathed in the same material whose plastic, salt-water resistant and insulating properties were a marvel of the age. It fostered a revolution in global communications and electrical power; but its history is also one of environmental disaster and colonial exploitation.

The sticky white latex of the Southeast Asian gutta-percha tree was traditionally collected from remote, hilly groves by workers scarring the living tree's bark with a knife – the latex is its natural defence, and can be collected by means of a quill channelled into a metal cup. The coagulated gutta-percha is softened and moulded in hot water and then, unlike India rubber (*Hevea brasiliensis* – see p. 47), it hardens into a material that survives immersion in the sea.

When, in the early 1850s, a hugely ambitious scheme was conceived to link the nerve centres of the British Empire by trans-oceanic electrical telegraphy, the demand for gutta-percha expanded to an industrial scale. Its exploitation became a matter of strategic global necessity for competing Western European powers who were hungry for news and for the political and commercial advantages of almost instant communications. Gutta-percha became a highly fashionable material and was used in the manufacture of golf balls, walking sticks and even furniture. Trees were felled, tapped and left to rot in their thousands, perhaps millions. It was an ecological catastrophe. Each specimen of the magnificent gutta-percha tree, which grows up to 30 metres (98 ft) tall, yields an average of just 11 ounces (312 g) of latex and does not become productive until about its thirtieth year. In Britain, imports of gutta-percha reached one million tons in 1875; in just two years, an estimated 69,000 trees were felled across Indonesia and Malaysia. Deforestation for cash crops is nothing new.[1]

Despite widespread establishment of plantations and more sustainable means of extraction, the survival of this remarkable tree was ensured only by the chemical synthesis of gutta-percha in the early twentieth century.

The pioneering Birch
Betula pendula; B. papyrifera

LOCAL NAMES: EUROPEAN WHITE BIRCH; WARTY BIRCH;
PAPER BIRCH; CANOE BIRCH (N. AMERICA)

OPPOSITE

Birch trees in autumn, Cairngorms
National Park, Scotland.

BELOW

Male birch catkins in spring.

In a broad band around the world's northern hemisphere, from Ireland to Kamchatka and from Alaska to Newfoundland, you will find the ubiquitous birch. In Europe and Asia the silver birch, with its slender trunk, pale ruptured bark, delicate leaves and catkins is a hardy pioneer; its tiny windborne seeds find a foothold on any bare or cleared ground. It grows quickly to a height of perhaps 25 metres (80 ft) but is no long-lived forest giant, surviving for not much more than 100 years. Its North American cousin, the paper birch, may grow taller, to 40 metres (130 ft) and is often found in the company of aspens and maples. It thrives on periodic forest fires, after which its seeds quickly colonize the freshly scorched earth.

In the end, both species are succeeded by the great forest canopy trees; but their winter hardiness ensures that they have few competitors in their most northerly ranges. Like maples, birch trees are adapted to extreme winters: in spring their roots generate positive water pressure to force out any air pockets left in cells after deep frosts. This drives sugars and water back up the tree – with the welcome by-product of a sweet sap that can be tapped to make a refreshing drink. Thin, horizontal scars visible on the trunk are lenticels: pores through which the tree exchanges gases with the atmosphere.

Birches are not just pioneers, but are trees of pioneers. They provide cover for mammals, birds and insects, lichens and fungi, allowing other, fruiting species to establish. Woodpeckers commonly nest in old birch trees. The resinous outer bark, which peels easily without harm to the tree, provides a very handy firelighter even when damp. In North America, indigenous communities valued paper birch bark above all for its use in making boxes and baskets and because, when removed in large sheets, it was the perfect material for roofing shelters and constructing lightweight, portable, waterproof and rough-hulled canoes.[2] Early European traders and fur trappers quickly adopted these canoes as their means of accessing the Great Lakes and rivers of the North. The wood and charcoal of both species is used as fuel, in making plywoods, especially for high quality drums, and as pulp for paper mills.

OPPOSITE

Gustav Klimt, *Birkenwald* (The Birch
Wood), 1903.

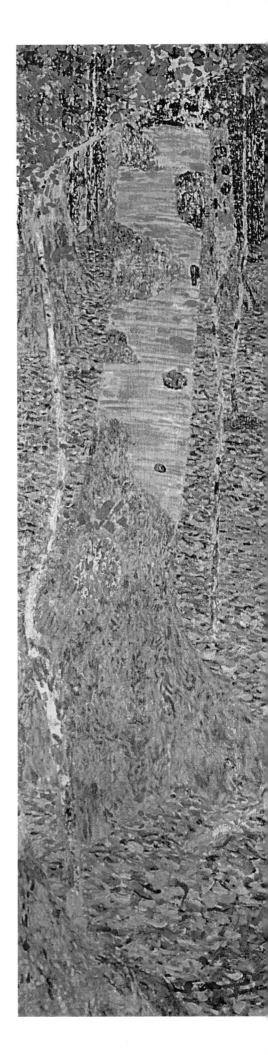

The magnificent Kapok
Ceiba pentandra

LOCAL NAMES: MUMIAN (CHINESE); YAXCHE (MAYAN);
KAPOKIER (FRENCH)

The kapok, or silk-cotton tree, may be best known for the fluffy fibres produced by its seed pods that catch the wind and ensure dispersal. Many a pillow and quilted jacket owes its soft warmth to this natural insulating material, although the naked fibres are irritating to eyes and skin. In its own right, though, the kapok is one of the most magnificent trees in the world. Its great height (up to 75 metres/250 ft), immense trunk and giant root buttresses make it a monument to nature, while its large, conical thorns are a menacing defence against attempts to climb it.

A deciduous tree of the South American tropics, now widely grown across similar latitudes around the world, the kapok was sacred to the Inca and Maya peoples, to whom it must have seemed like a stairway to the skies and to the centre of the earth. It is sometimes called the castle of the devil; even so, it is often planted close to villages and to temples. The kapok is the national emblem of no fewer than three countries: Guatemala, Puerto Rico and Equatorial Guinea. In Freetown, Sierra Leone, a prized specimen is regarded as a symbol of freedom.

A mature tree may produce 300 to 400 pods annually.[3] The seeds are harvested and then dried, when they open to produce the soft springy fibres used widely as padding, in upholstery and as an insulator, although their flammability poses a fire risk. Indigenous peoples of the Amazon basin wrap the fibres around their poisonous blow darts to make an airtight seal. The seeds produce an edible oil that can also be used as a fuel and in paint mixing. The bark yields a diuretic and diabetes treatment; the light, buoyant wood is used for making canoes and for carving, while the foul-smelling flowers attract bats and other pollinators. Such a large, architecturally complex tree inevitably forms its own biome, hosting a range of species from amphibians to insects, mammals, birds and reptiles.

The kapok belongs to the *Bombax* genus, which includes the water chestnut and two other giants, balsa and baobab. It is related to, but distinct from, the wild kapok (*Bombax valetonii*), a native of Southeast Asia.

Hazelnut
Corylus avellana

LOCAL NAMES: WALKING-STICK TREE

Hazel is the woodsman's tree par excellence. From Britain to the Ural mountains and as far south as Cyprus, this attractive but modest-sized multi-stemmed species, rarely growing more than 10 metres (33 ft) tall, graces Europe's ancient woodlands. The hazel is one of the earliest woodland trees to burst into springtime activity. From February onwards, its pale-yellow, drooping male catkins brighten the short days, offering pollen up to the tiny red flowers on its speckled pale-brown, smooth twigs.

Hazels come into leaf in March and grow at prodigious speed throughout the summer – sometimes well over a metre in a year. Given enough sun they produce abundant crops of small round nuts, appearing creamy green in their hat-like bracts (*haesel* is the Old English word for a cap) and then ripen to a dark shiny brown. They can be eaten while unripe; in autumn they are collected

ABOVE

The distinctive green bracts around the nuts explain the name: Old English *'haesel'*, meaning 'cap'.

OPPOSITE

Male hazelnut catkins hang heavy with pollen in spring.

by both humans and squirrels, who cache them as a vital winter food source. Cultivated varieties include cobnuts and filberts.

Hazels followed close behind birch trees in colonizing northern latitudes after the last Ice Age and it seems likely that they were propagated as much by hunter-gatherer communities following herds of elk and deer as they were by industrious squirrels. Just as important as the nuts, the strong, pliable rods that spontaneously sprout from the base of the tree are perfect for all sorts of light construction and tool-making. The woven rods make strong, lightweight hurdles for animal pens and fencing; they formed wall panels for traditional round houses and wattles for medieval buildings, daubed with clay, straw and dung to make them weatherproof. They were used to improvise stretching frames and sprung devices, as handles for brooms, and were bundled as faggots for firing ovens.

The hazel is naturally self-coppicing and it must have been a prime mentor in the education of early woodsmen. They realized its potential for producing regular crops of straight, even-bored poles that could be harvested every seven or eight years on a continuous, ever-giving cycle. Hazel rods are found on archaeological sites wherever wet soils preserve wood: in ancient causeways across marshes; in the structures of crannogs (loch-dwellings). And in the very earliest inhabited structures of Scotland and Northern England hazelnut shells are found, carbonized, in the long-dead embers of campfires.

Balsa
Ochroma lagopus; O. pyramidale

LOCAL NAMES: BOIS FLOT (FRENCH); BALSO TAMBOR
(SPANISH)

When, in 1947, the Norwegian explorer Thor Heyerdahl mounted an expedition to test his theory that Polynesia had been colonized from South America, there was only one choice of wood for building the hull of his boat. In Spanish *balsa* means, literally, 'raft'. Early Pacific navigators must have had an intimate knowledge of trees and their timbers, along with all sorts of practical uses for woody materials, while early Spanish colonizers had written of the outstanding abilities of native craft.[4] Heyerdahl, too, used the best materials available for such a long voyage: balsa logs for the hull; bamboo and banana leaves for the cabin; mangrove and fir for the steering oar; pine for the centre boards. After 101 days at sea *Kon-Tiki* made landfall with a bump on a then-uninhabited atoll, Raroia, in the Tuamotu Islands, 4,300 miles (6,900 km) from its port of departure in Callao, Peru. The hull of the raft had been constructed from nine 60-centimetre (2 ft) thick balsa logs, which proved uniquely effective in not only providing buoyancy but also riding waves, allowing wash to drain as if through a sieve.

The unique properties of balsa wood had already been proven in the equally demanding aerial environment of the Second World War: it was used in the airframe of the plywood-clad de Havilland Mosquito, the 'wooden wonder', giving it sufficient strength and lightness to attain high speeds and altitude as a multi-purpose combat aircraft. Latter-day enthusiasts have often made models of the sleek Mosquito using similar materials to the original, glued together with balsa cement in time-honoured fashion.

The secret of balsa, according to Dr Roger Heady who has studied its properties using a Scanning Electron Microscope, is that only about 40 per cent of its volume is solid: the rest is air.[5] The lofty balsa tree is held up by hydraulic pressure inside very thin-walled vessels, and although technically a hardwood, when dry it has a density of just under 9 kilos (20 lb) per cubic metre – nearly one-sixth that of oak. It is a native of the humid tropical forests of South and Central America, growing as much as 27 metres (90 ft) in less than fifteen years, but with a lifespan of little more than thirty to forty years.

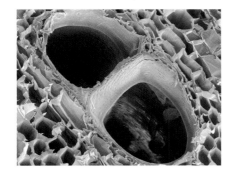

White mulberry
Morus alba

LOCAL NAMES: SANG (CHINESE)

In early October 1889 Vincent van Gogh, while a patient at St Rémy asylum in Provence, was enchanted by the rich autumn foliage of a white mulberry. The expressionistic exuberance and vitality of the painting made it one of his own favourite studies, despite the mental anguish that so preoccupied him during that year.

Chinese artists were celebrating the beauties of the mulberry many centuries before the Dutch master. This iconic tree is the favoured food of the silkworm, the larva of the silk moth (*Bombix mori*) which emerges from a cocoon of this uniquely light, thin and valuable yarn. One of the finest natural fabrics, silk was first recorded in the fourth millennium BCE. The first text on the cultivation of the white mulberry was written two centuries before the birth of Christ. Silk production was the preserve of a Chinese élite who jealously guarded the secret of its manufacture. Silk cloth was known to, and prized by, the ancient merchants of Greece, Rome and the Middle East, traded along the legendary Silk Road and brought home by campaigning soldiers. Only in the reign of the Byzantine Emperor Justinian (527–565 CE) was the biology and technology of silk production first understood and copied in Europe.

The tree on which the silk moth lays its eggs has a domed profile, with heart-shaped leaves growing densely on upwardly spreading branches. Although modest in height at up to 20 metres (65 ft) tall, it is fast growing and long- lived – perhaps surviving for two thousand years and more. The tree, now widely cultivated across the world, is deciduous in temperate regions and evergreen in the tropics. In spring male catkins violently expel pollen – apparently at half the speed of sound.

The purple, red or white fruits are edible and sweet. The leaves can be fed to livestock or infused as a tea and an extract has proved effective as a treatment for snakebites. The bark of the root has antibacterial and possibly anti-carcino-genic properties. Fibre can be extracted from the bark while the wood, with its dark brown heart and much paler sapwood, is hard and rot-resistant. The same attractions that inspired van Gogh make the mulberry a favourite ornamental tree of parks and gardens.

1

2

3

4

A. *Guajacum officinale L.*

Echter Guajakbaum.

F. Kirchner sc.

Tree of life: Lignum vitae
Guaiacum officinale; G. sanctum

LOCAL NAMES: PALO SANTO (SPANISH); POCKHOLTZ; IRONWOOD

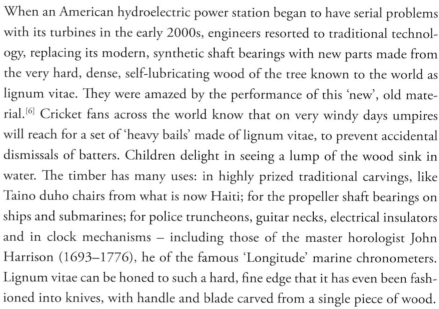

When an American hydroelectric power station began to have serial problems with its turbines in the early 2000s, engineers resorted to traditional technology, replacing its modern, synthetic shaft bearings with new parts made from the very hard, dense, self-lubricating wood of the tree known to the world as lignum vitae. They were amazed by the performance of this 'new', old material.[6] Cricket fans across the world know that on very windy days umpires will reach for a set of 'heavy bails' made of lignum vitae, to prevent accidental dismissals of batters. Children delight in seeing a lump of the wood sink in water. The timber has many uses: in highly prized traditional carvings, like Taino duho chairs from what is now Haiti; for the propeller shaft bearings on ships and submarines; for police truncheons, guitar necks, electrical insulators and in clock mechanisms – including those of the master horologist John Harrison (1693–1776), he of the famous 'Longitude' marine chronometers. Lignum vitae can be honed to such a hard, fine edge that it has even been fashioned into knives, with handle and blade carved from a single piece of wood.

The two species of Caribbean evergreens from which the wood is cut are slow-growing and unimpressive in size – no more than 10 metres (33ft) tall with small, compound leaves, but the delicate purple/white bloom is the national flower of Jamaica. Resin from the bark is traditionally used in the treatment of several conditions, including coughs and arthritis, while its wood chips can be made into an infusion and drunk as a tea. Because of historic over-exploitation, *guaiacum* is now listed as an endangered species, its export restricted.

Lignum vitae's fascinating properties come with equally heavy historical baggage. The first specimen seen in Britain was acquired in 1687 by the Irish physician and collector Hans Sloane. (Sloane's collections – which included plant specimens and animal skeletons as well as manuscripts, drawings and coins – would provide the foundation of the British Museum, and, later, the Natural History Museum.) The wood became a valuable part of the exploitative transatlantic 'triangular' trade in slaves, plantation produce, native crafts and natural resources.

Beech
Fagus sylvatica; F. grandifolia

LOCAL NAMES: EUROPEAN BEECH; AMERICAN BEECH

From Ireland to the Black Sea and from Scandinavia to the toe of Italy, the soaring columns and translucent emerald canopies of beech trees furnish Europe's great forests. The eastern half of North America has its own, closely related beech; Asia too is home to members of the same family, the *Fagaceae*. The beech is no shy creature: it demands space and light and is greedy for both, shading out competition from other trees and shrubs. Below ground, the beech develops an intimate association with mycorrhizal fungi, sharing sugars in return for nitrogen and other scarce minerals. Beech forests are gregarious communities of mutual interest and solidarity.

Like the oaks, beech trees produce very large crops of nuts – or mast – two or three for every spiky husk; and, like the oaks, they do so irregularly. In mast years, superabundance ensures that not all are eaten by hungry birds and mammals. Beech woods were invaluable in traditional communities: each autumn, pigs would be turned into the woods to fatten on the nuts – a practice called pannage – before winter slaughtering. The nuts are oil rich and very good to eat; they can also be roasted as a coffee substitute. The wood of the beech, which is strong and dense with a fine grain, is used in furniture making, for turning on lathes and for flooring. Thin boards were once used to bind manuscripts – the English word 'book' comes from Old English 'boc', the name for a beech. The wood produces a fine charcoal that burns long and hot, leaving a tarry residue used as a waterproofing and preservative paint. The leaves can be cut and used as fodder for cattle and the bark contains tannin, used in curing leather.

Beech trees, which generally grow to more than 30 metres (98 ft) tall, also coppice well, producing regular crops of poles and fuel. With a tendency to hang on to many of their dried leaves through winter, they make highly effective hedging plants. But, unlike oaks, they do not live to a great age – rarely more than 250 years; and that may explain the relative paucity of beech-derived names in old settlements, in ancient boundary clauses and estate texts.

Small-leaved lime
Tilia cordata

LOCAL NAMES: PRY

When, in the old English epic poem, Beowulf faced the ultimate challenge – a vengeful dragon – the linden-wood shield, which had protected the warrior in many a combat, proved insufficient and an iron shield was required. For mere mortals, including the Anglo-Saxon king Rædwald (died *c.*625), whose burial at Sutton Hoo in a great ship is one of the glories of English archaeology, linden – or lime – wood was the material of choice for a battle shield: light, gleamingly pale, strong and able to absorb the energy of a deadly blow.

The small-leaved lime, or pry, is a splendid, spreading tree growing to 40 metres (130 ft) and native to most of Europe. Now rarer than in Rædwald's day, it was once a very common tree of woodland, heath and coppice, and is fossilized in many 'linden' place names. Lime poles are still found holding up the mud-daubed panels of medieval walls. Grinling Gibbons (1648–1721) was fond of the wood for his ornate carvings, and many a medieval altarpiece, now dark-stained and deeply polished, was cut from a pry. Its clean, even grain and lightness make it ideal for instrument sounding boards and piano keys. It makes fine charcoal, too.

Wood is not the lime's only produce: the inner bark, or bast, was for centuries stripped, beaten and twisted to make a strong rope, and modern reconstructions of Viking Age ocean-going craft still use lime-bast for their cordage. The leaves, when young and fresh, are edible and can be used as fodder. The abundant pale-cream flowers attract bees, and lime honey is highly prized.

The small-leaved lime may grow to a great age: specimens of 700 to 800 years or more have been recorded, although dating them precisely is difficult because the mature heartwood rots from inside out and few complete growth-ring sequences have been found. An elegant, ornamental tree, the lime lined famous boulevards such as the grand *Unter den Linden* in Berlin. Its original trees were planted in 1647, while the existing specimens date from the 1950s. The iconic street sign was looted by British soldiers in 1945 and is now kept in London's Imperial War Museum.

Calabash
Crescentia cujete

LOCAL NAMES: CUITÉ (BRAZILIAN); CALABACERO (SPANISH)

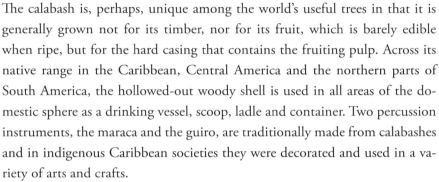

OPPOSITE

Harvesting calabash fruit, *c.*1880.

BELOW

Ripening calabash fruits planted in Gardens by the Bay nature park, Singapore.

The calabash is, perhaps, unique among the world's useful trees in that it is generally grown not for its timber, nor for its fruit, which is barely edible when ripe, but for the hard casing that contains the fruiting pulp. Across its native range in the Caribbean, Central America and the northern parts of South America, the hollowed-out woody shell is used in all areas of the domestic sphere as a drinking vessel, scoop, ladle and container. Two percussion instruments, the maraca and the guiro, are traditionally made from calabashes and in indigenous Caribbean societies they were decorated and used in a variety of arts and crafts.

The calabash is an adaptable tree, growing in patches of waste ground, woodland margins, roadsides and coastal scrub. It is drought- and damp-tolerant and hardy. Growing to 10 metres (33 ft) tall with a thin trunk and spreading canopy, when mature it may flower all year round, with greenish-yellow, purple-veined blooms that are said to smell like cabbage. The distinctive fruits take several months to develop and can grow as large as 25 centimetres (10 in) across. The pulp is valued as an astringent and laxative and a syrup made from it is used to relieve the symptoms of colds and fevers. It is also said to be an abortifacient.[7] The leaves, occasionally added to soups, are made into an infusion to clean wounds and promote healing, while the bark may have antibacterial properties. The seeds from the fruit are cooked and can be eaten or used as an aromatic coffee substitute. Fibres from the inner bark were used to make rope, while the wood was split and shaved into laths to make baskets.[8]

The Taino people of Hispaniola – now Haiti and the Dominican Republic – used the hollowed calabash, complete with eye holes, as a hunting mask. Smaller shells might be filled with beans or rice and made into maracas, while larger shells were hollowed and grooved to make the guiro, the forerunner of the skiffle band's washboard. In Africa, another calabash – not a true tree but a vine known as the bottle gourd (*Lagenaria siceraria*) – is made into an even greater variety of percussion instruments, including the xylophone-like balafon, and it forms the sound box of the 'African harp' or Kora.

Cork oak
Quercus suber

LOCAL NAMES: SOBREIRO (PORTUGUESE); CHÊNE-LIÈGE (FRENCH)

It is not the toothed evergreen leaves or the bizarre and unique deeply fissured bark of the cork tree that allow botanists to place it in the oak family. Only the acorn, rich in tannins and beloved of autumn-grazing pigs, offers a clue to the untrained eye. A medium-sized tree growing to about 20 metres (66 ft), the cork oak is superbly adapted to coastal Mediterranean lands with hot summers and cool, moist winters. The thick, insulating bark is highly resistant to the periodic bush fires so common in its native habitat extending from Sicily in the east and the Pyrenees in the northwest to Algeria and Morocco in the south and west. In its heartlands of Portugal and western Spain, open cork forests have been carefully managed over many generations to produce a unique biome, the *montado* or *dehesa*, wood pasture rich in flora and fauna.[9] Cork oak forests are the last bastion of that precious cat, the Iberian lynx, while in Morocco they support the Barbary macaque and short-toed eagle.

Very few trees will survive the complete removal of their outer bark, which protects the crucial living vessels that transport sugars, minerals and water between leaves and roots. Once mature, at about twenty-five years of age, the cork tolerates this apparent vandalism and can be harvested every seven to ten years, surviving perhaps 250 years as a productive tree. The older the tree and the bigger its diameter, the more lucrative the harvest.

Cork is a fine, breathable, buoyant natural insulator, most famously used for wine corks but also as flooring, as the core of cricket balls, for fishing floats and in soundproofing. But without the wine industry's continued use of this superbly sustainable natural material the cork forests and their special ecologies may not survive.

The cork is monoecious, with separate male and female flowers on the same tree, and is wind pollinated. New trees are grown from acorns and, such is the inherent genetic diversity of the species, local and marginal populations are highly valued for their variability – in the Mamora forest of Morocco, for example, the acorns are said to be edible.[10] In most areas of commercial cultivation both the tree and the forests that it dominates are protected by law.

The Rubber tree
Hevea brasiliensis

LOCAL NAMES: SIRINGA (SPANISH); PARÁ RUBBER;
SERIGUEIRA (PORTUGUESE)

The intense exploitation of the world's natural resources has now escalated into a deadly competition. When Chico Mendes was murdered in 1988 the plight of Brazil's traditional rubber tappers, and of the Amazon rainforest, made global headlines. Mendes had organized his fellow workers to protest against the clearing of productive rainforest for cattle grazing – that is, for the world beef industry. His legacy was a government agreement to set aside 'extractive reserves' where the sustainable harvesting of the forest's bounty was protected.[11]

Two thousand years before the arrival of European entrepreneurs in the New World, the Olmec (the name means, literally, 'rubber people') were using the remarkable sticky latex of the rubber tree and another species, *Castilla elastica*, to make balls for their ritual games. Their successors in Central America, the Maya and Aztecs, used it to waterproof fabric and for making containers. Samples were first introduced to the European scientific community in the middle of the eighteenth century by Charles Marie de La Condamine. The English scientist Joseph Priestley discovered its value in rubbing out pencil script; and François Fresneau identified turpentine as its solvent. It was first vulcanized, for durability, by Charles Goodyear in 1839, but not until forty years later were large numbers of seeds smuggled illegally out of Brazil by Henry Wickham and delivered to Kew Gardens: the precursor to vast plantations in the British Indian colonies. Rubber has never looked back.

The deciduous native tree grows to a height of up to 40 metres (130 feet). Like the gutta-percha it exudes sticky latex when the bark is cut or incised. The milky liquid is collected and processed into myriad applications: in vehicle tyres, clothing, shoes, insulators, shock-absorbers and more. In smaller cultivated trees latex production declines after about thirty years and the trees are felled for timber, used in furniture making and as fuel. Seeds are produced copiously and are pressed into oil and seedcake as an animal feed supplement. The inevitable tensions between global commercial interests and local, sustainable cropping of rubber are a test of natural and human resilience and of the international community's ability to manage and protect these critical resources for the future.

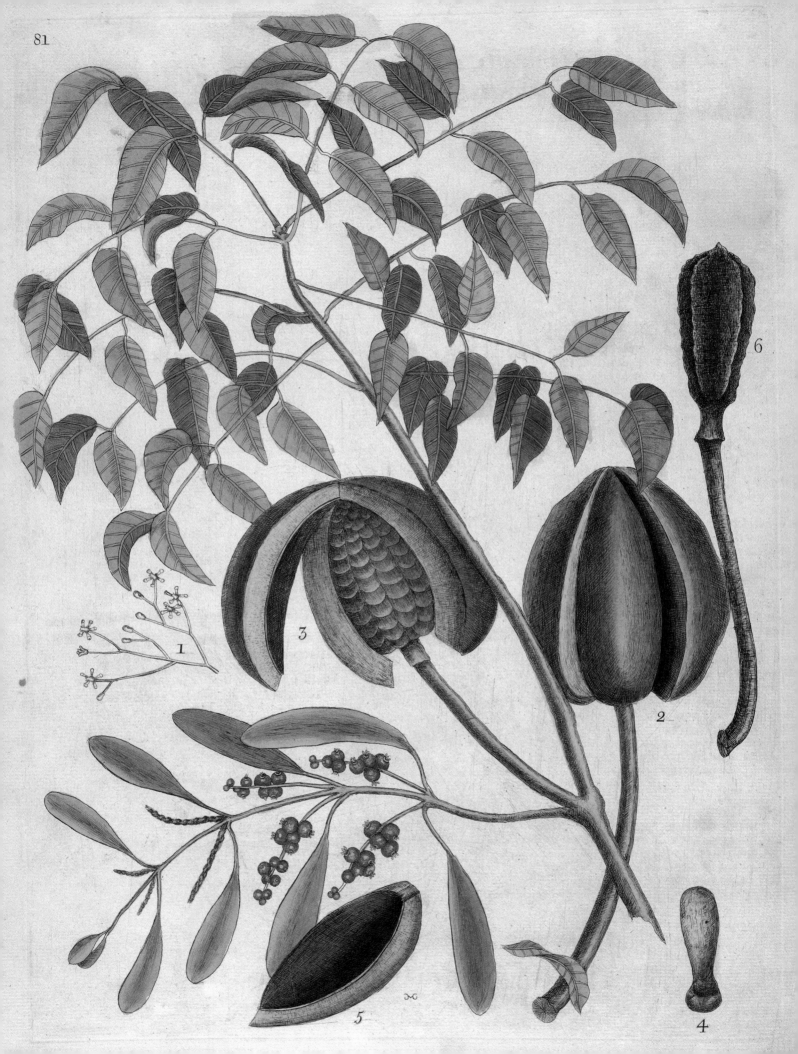

Mahogany
Swietenia mahagoni and S. macrophylla

LOCAL NAMES: AMERICAN MAHOGANY; WEST INDIAN MAHOGANY

In the tropical forests of West Africa, M'oganwo (*Khaya senegalensis*) is, literally, 'king of trees'. When slaves were first taken from there to the Caribbean they found trees whose timber had the same characteristics of dense, richly coloured dark grain, superb durability, easy working and surprising lightness. Two of the most globally important timber trees have, ever since, been known as mahogany.

European entrepreneurs very quickly found a lucrative market for the timber in Europe. By the mid-eighteenth century, it is said, half a million feet of mahogany planks were being shipped annually from Jamaica. The trees had been felled, logged and sawn by cheap, exploited labour.[12] Some of this wood was used in early colonial Caribbean architecture. The interior of the Cathedral of Santa María la Menor in Santo Domingo (Dominican Republic), the oldest surviving church in the West Indies, boasts an interior ornamented with mahogany carvings from before 1540.[13] Much of the commercial trade was destined for European shipbuilding; but mahogany's reputation as the paramount wood for fine furniture ensured that by the twentieth century it was threatened with extinction outside plantations.

The two Caribbean species are members, like the Indian neem (see Chapter 2, p. 89) and the West African *Khaya*, of the *Meliaceae* family, mostly evergreens and all natives of the tropics. The true mahoganies grow to about 30 metres (98 ft) in height in their natural state, with a single-stemmed, slightly fluted trunk and broad, shady canopy. Timber aside, the bark contains tannins used in leather curing and, for its astringent properties, it is widely used as an antiseptic and fever-medicine and in the treatment of diarrhoea. An oil can be extracted from the seeds, while the crushed fruit shells are used as a potting medium. Interplanted with coffee and other cash crops, the mahogany provides quick-growing shade. The backs and sides of many of the celebrated Martin acoustic guitars are made with mahogany for its rich decorative patterning and stiff resonance.

Paper mulberry
Broussonetia papyrifera

LOCAL NAMES: SAA (THAI); TAPA CLOTH TREE; HIAPO (TONGA)

OPPOSITE

The leaves and flowers of the paper
mulberry tree, from a botanical illustration
that appeared in an encyclopedia
published in Vienna in 1817.

BELOW

Paper mulberry: leaf detail.

BOTTOM

The flowers of paper mulberry have
anemone-like tendrils.

For some, the saa or paper mulberry is an untidy eyesore and conservationists consider it a potentially invidious weed. But across Southeast Asia and the Pacific archipelagos it is a hugely valuable resource, principally in the production of paper and cloth. One of the principal hypotheses for the human colonization of the Pacific from a single point of origin – the so-called 'Out of Taiwan' model – is supported by the genetic footprint of the paper mulberry in its various hybrids found across the Philippines and the Pacific.

The saa, as it is known in Thai, is a relative of those other 'hardware store' trees, the breadfruit and jackfruit (see Chapter 5, pp. 201 and 213). It grows quickly and variably, up to 15 metres (50 ft) in height, with sprawling branches and deciduous foliage.[14] The strong but pliable fibres of the inner bark were being used to make cloth in the Pearl River delta of China some 8,000 years ago. Strips of the bark are traditionally beaten together after being peeled from a living tree, to soften and thin them before decorative paints are added in distinct local designs. The bare trunk is then protected by wrapping it in leaves until the bark, like cork, regrows. In the collections of the botanical gardens at Kew in London is an example of such 'tapa' cloth made by the wife of one of the mutineers from HMAT *Bounty*.[15]

The spread of early Chinese civilization is partly credited to the production of paper, around or before 100 BCE, made from the saa by pounding and mixing the inner bark with water to create a pulp which was then spread on a mesh until dry.[16] Rope and cord, those essentials for maritime exploration and sea fishing, are traditionally made from the roots of the saa. The fruit and leaves are edible and both are used in traditional medicine. Widely planted for its produce and a feature of city streets because of its tolerance of pollution, this important tree is also blamed for high levels of allergies on account of its prolific pollen production.

Candlenut
Aleurites moluccana

LOCAL NAMES: INDIAN WALNUT; KEMIRI (MALAY); VARNISH TREE; KUKUI (HAWAIIAN)

Some 13,000 years ago, while Northern Europe was still blanketed by an ice sheet, the inhabitants of Timor, in eastern Indonesia, were harvesting the nuts, leaves and wood of the candlenut tree. It provided light and food, medicines, dyes and inks, and they used the timber to build canoes. Across the Pacific Ocean traditional island communities have, ever since, relied on this remarkable tree to sustain their livelihoods.

Often found growing with multiple trunks – perhaps the result of former coppicing – the candlenut may grow to 30 metres (98 feet) tall with a great, spreading canopy of dense foliage. The large leaves, distinctively pale underneath, are either heart-shaped or three-toed. Clusters of white blooms, similar in appearance to elderflowers, are followed by green fruits the size of large plums or small apples. Inside is a creamy, knobbly nut, like a large hazelnut and very oily. Roasted and pounded, it is cooked in sauces with vegetables and rice – although in various parts of the world, the nuts are more or less toxic, with a strong laxative effect. The nuts are also pierced and threaded onto sticks to be used as convenient, long-lasting torches. They can be pressed to release oil for lighting, soap-making and preserving wood. The seed cake can then be processed to make a snack or to be used as a fertilizer.[17] Hawaiian fisherman are said to spit the nut's juice onto water to break its surface tension so that they can see fish below.[18] The oil has sometimes been used as a biodiesel fuel. The inner bark of the candlenut yields a red dye for colouring tapa cloth (see Paper mulberry, p. 51), while the wood is used for carving and to make parts for canoes.

Across the Pacific, islanders rely on the candlenut for a range of medicinal applications: the oil as a purgative; the bark to treat wounds, dysentery and tumours; the leaves to treat constipation and the nuts as a laxative or, pulped, in poultices for headaches and gonorrhoea. Such traditional uses persist but are not always supported by hard scientific evidence.

Royal palm
Roystonea regia

LOCAL NAMES: CUBAN ROYAL PALM

It is easy to dismiss ornamental trees as no more than a landscape gardener's decorative motif, but there's no doubting the aesthetic impact of a road or plaza lined with magnificent royal palms. Slim columnar trunks arch into a deep azure sky while luxurious fronds bend like sails to the wind. The royal palm, a native of the Caribbean and of Florida, belongs more to the world of gardening or architecture, perhaps, than to forestry; and, strictly speaking, palms are not trees at all. But these palms function in just the same way as trees in the environment: framing city streets and buildings and inspiring the soaring vaults of cathedrals. They often stand sentinel on hillsides or grace that liminal space between earth, sky and water.

The royal palm, whose natural environment is tropical wetland margins, becomes, when brought into city, town or formal garden, a temple column, a flagpole, a uniformed soldier on parade; a functionary of ordered space. In Cuba the tree plays an important role in popular religious culture and, being a palm, it has other uses, too. In the wild, the fresh apical buds of saplings are plucked and eaten as a delicacy (killing the young tree in the process). The leaves, at a hefty 50 pounds (22 kilos) a time, will give a passer-by a nasty injury when shed from a height of over 33 metres (100 ft). But they make fine thatching and the stems are used in the construction of furniture. Fibres from the leaf sheath may prove to have applications in lightweight composite alternatives to plastics. The trunks, not true wood but just as tough and flexible, are sawn into planks like hardwood timber and used in construction, for making rot-resistant piles for wharves, and in canoe building.[19]

Unlike the date palm, the fruits of the *Roystonea regia*, hanging in great bunches from the crown, are not generally edible; but oil is extracted from them for animal feed. The roots are used as a diuretic while according to a growing number of scientific studies, a lipid extract of the fruit has an inhibiting effect on the male age-related condition of an enlarged prostate gland.[20] One way or another, the royal palm is a useful tree.

CHAPTER 2

Dragon's Blood and Jesuit's Bark: trees for dyes, perfumes and medicine

OPPOSITE
Prizing dragon's blood resin from a tree
trunk on the island of Socotra, south of the
Arabian Peninsula.

ACROSS THE WORLD, THE SCIENTIFIC SEARCH IS ON FOR ever more potent drugs to cure complex diseases, to replace those whose targets have become resistant or which are proving intractable to conventional therapies. A parallel movement, whose adherents range from homeopaths to organic gardeners and hedgerow foragers, draws on folkloric wisdom to extract medicines, tonics, skin conditioners, dyes and 'natural' cosmetics from all sorts of plants, many of them trees.

The trees included in this chapter have stories to tell of traditional medicines and processes, of colonial exploitation, of marvellous life-changing discoveries. Treatments for malaria, scurvy, cancer, intestinal worms and all sorts of chronic and acute conditions have been derived from trees, particularly their leaves and bark, for millennia. Others, like the anti-carcinogenic Pacific yew, have given up their secrets only in recent decades. Many tree extracts have antibacterial, antioxidant, astringent and purgative properties and the seed oils of an increasing number of species are showing remarkable applications in treating blood-sugar disorders such as diabetes. The discovery of spectacular dyes led to the formation of whole nations and to jealously guarded monopolies, even to a search for the blood of a mythical dragon. Some of the world's most valuable and exotic trees have been driven to the edge of extinction by over-exploitation – only to be rescued, and then consigned to obscurity by the invention of synthesized chemical paints and dyes. Tannin, produced by many trees as a natural defence against insect attack and concentrated in leaves and bark, has an enduring role in the traditional preparation of leather. Other volatile substances produce natural perfumes and insect repellents.

The reputations of some trees have risen and fallen as their supposed virtues have been exposed as fraudulent or over-optimistic; others are ever-present in our medicine cabinets. Aspirin, the little white pill once derived from the bark of the white willow, underwent a long period of refinement because of its naturally deleterious side effects caused by natural extracts from the bark. And readers may be surprised by the exclusion of one or two very obvious trees.

Ginkgo biloba, the maidenhair tree, one of the world's most exotic and ancient species, yields the most commercially successful herbal remedies in the world. And yet, since there is not the slightest scientific evidence for its efficacy, it has been pruned from this selection. In contrast, the humble sea buckthorn must once have been the go-to shrub for coastal communities getting through the lean months of winter – these days, most people wouldn't even know what it looks like.

Many trees that play pivotal roles in their communities providing a huge range of assets, from shade to timber to animal fodder and edible fruits, have also acquired reputations for being able to cure almost any malady, from sexually transmitted diseases to the common cold. Sometimes, science has proved folklore right; in other cases, the jury is more sceptical. Many substances yielded by trees are poisonous in high doses – some lethally so. Global knowledge of nature's curative and chemical wonders has come at the inevitable experimental price of all those known and unknown victims who suffered in the cause of learning.

One thing is for sure, humans have not yet discovered all the chemical and medicinal treasures of the natural world; the search goes on to see what might yet be out there hiding in plain sight. Some unfashionable, neglected communities whose survival and health depends on trees hold knowledge that may yet give up important secrets – a reminder that traditional societies are as resourceful and adaptable as the trees with whom they share their lives.

Aromatic frankincense
Boswellia sacra

LOCAL NAMES: OLIBANUM; LEVONA (HEBREW); MOGAR (ARABIC); RUXIANG (CHINESE)

Three magi came out of the East, bearing gifts for the infant Jesus and, as every Christian nativity play actor knows, one of these gifts was exotic frankincense. The aromatic resin makes its first literary appearance in the Book of Exodus, burned as a sacred symbolic perfume of the divine; and one suspects an origin as a shamanic trance-inducer or ritual cleansing fumigant. Images of the resin being transported in sacks can be found in Egyptian murals from the second millennium BCE. The resin is soluble in alcohol, while an essential oil, used in anointing ceremonies and aromatherapy, is produced by distillation and used in Chinese medicine to treat diabetes. The name frankincense (*franc* meaning 'pure' in medieval French) was a guarantee of quality, suggesting a parallel trade in inferior or adulterated rival products.

In the thirteenth century, production was described by a Chinese writer, Zhao Ruga,[1] who correctly identified its origin in the territories of the Horn of Africa. He related how it was obtained by notching the trunk of a tree with a hatchet to allow the pinous resin to flow out. The resin, hardened into lumps, was transported by elephant to the coast and taken by sea to a trading centre in Sumatra.

The tree that produces this divine substance is *Boswellia sacra* or one of its very close relatives, an unprepossessing, scrubby deciduous bush with peeling, papery bark but startling yellow and orange flowers. It grows in Somalia, which dominates world production of incense, and Oman and Yemen on the Arabian peninsula. One of nature's survivors, it grows in bare, steep, often drought-ridden places, clinging tenaciously to exposed rocks and perhaps collecting vital moisture from coastal fogs. By far the majority of the frankincense collected – several thousand tons per year – is sold to the Catholic or Orthodox Christian churches for use in censers. Today, the tree is regarded as a threatened species, over-exploited and vulnerable to attack by the longhorn beetle. Sacred to so many historic religions, the frankincense deserves to be protected as a cultured treasure as well as a botanical curiosity.

Little white pill: White willow
Salix alba

LOCAL NAMES: CRICKET-BAT WILLOW

OPPOSITE

Leaves, twigs, flowers and catkins of the white willow, after Hempel & Wilhelm, 1889.

BELOW

The pliant stems of the white willow are used in traditional basketry, and pollarded specimens are often to be seen lining lowland rivers and dykes, where they are regularly harvested for their thin rods, called withies. White willow produces a fine-grained charcoal used in the manufacture of gunpowder and artists' pencils.

OVERLEAF

Pollarded white willows at sunrise, Lower Saxony, Germany.

On 2 June 1763 a letter, written by the Rev. Edward Stone (1702–68) of Charlton-on-Otmoor, Oxfordshire was read to the Royal Society in London. It began:

> *Among the many useful discoveries which this age hath made, there are very few which better deserve the attention of the public… There is a bark of an English tree, which I have found by experience to be a powerful astringent, and very efficacious in curing aguish and intermitting disorders.* [2]

Stone, it seems, was suffering the symptoms of malaria (see Cinchona, p. 81) and, on finding that eating a small quantity of the bark of the white willow relieved his symptoms, he experimented with drying, grinding, storing it and dosing himself with varying amounts to record its effects. Satisfied, he tried it on fifty of his parishioners who complained of 'agues' or fevers, with considerable success. Stone had rediscovered salicylate, known to ancients such as Pliny and Hippocrates but more or less ignored by the medical profession for a millennium or so. Stone's bark exhibited unpleasant side effects such as stomach irritation and even bleeding, so the hunt was on for a more benign extract. Only in 1897 was salicylic acid successfully synthesized and marketed by the German dye manufacturers Bayer, under the name Aspirin.

Stone's bark came from the white willow, one of several species of the family *Salicaceae* native to Europe and East Asia. It is a tall spreading tree (up to 30 metres/98 ft) with characteristic leaning boughs and cascades of long, thin sharply pointed leaves whose undersides are a pale whitish green. The bark is distinctively fissured. The wood, which is light, strong and supple, is most famously used for making cricket bats. The active ingredient in Aspirin is a plant hormone that encourages root formation and growth – like most willows, *Salix alba* will 'strike': that is, a green twig or stick from one of its branches will grow into a new tree when planted in soil, and as a result it is one of the most easily propagated of all trees.

Haematoxylon campechianum.

F. Guimpel fec.

Pirates and nations: the Logwood
Haematoxylum campechianum

LOCAL NAMES: CAMPECHE; BLOODWOOD; JAMAICA WOOD

Not many trees can be said to have given birth to an entire nation. Belize, formerly British Honduras, was an early colonial possession in Central America, violently wrested from the Mayan empire, its indigenous forest tribes displaced by settlers and pirates, who came to be known as Baymen, from about 1638 onwards. Over two centuries a territory was carved out to control and exploit large-scale export of the small, leguminous logwood tree, its heartwood containing a brilliant purple-red or dark black dye used on fabrics and paper. The dye became so precious in the seventeenth and eighteenth centuries that it supported a pirate colony and fostered continuing wars between British and Spanish fleets. Large numbers of African and Caribbean slaves were taken to Honduras to work in logging and debarking settlements, and a sorry history of violence, disease, malnutrition and abuse followed. From 1862 the region centred on the logging settlements became a Crown Colony, achieving independence as the Republic of Belize in 1981 (with still-unresolved claims on its territory by neighbouring Guatemala). A logwood tree, flanked by black and white loggers, features on the country's flag.

The logwood grows from 9 to 13 metres (29 to 42 ft), with pea-like leaves and yellow flowers (the giveaway traits of a legume) and a spreading canopy. The trunk is distinctively fluted, like a cathedral column. It grows in lowland areas close to rivers and lagoons and was easily transported along the region's rivers to coastal ports for shipment. A transatlantic cargo shipment brought traders £100 per ton in the seventeenth century, and the wood was still exported in quantity even after the introduction of synthetic dyes from the 1850s onwards. The logs, which begin to exude the unprocessed haematoxylin immediately on cutting, were chipped and the chips boiled under pressure to release soluble resins and essential oils.[3] At one time the dye was used as a sort of litmus reagent for acids and alkalis. Natural haematoxylin is still used in histological research as a stain. Belize's rich biological diversity, with 60 per cent forest cover, is recognized as a globally valuable natural heritage asset: part of the Mesoamerican Biological Corridor.

The real thing? Dragon's blood tree
Dracaena cinnabari

LOCAL NAMES: SOCOTRA DRAGON TREE; A'ARHIYIB (ARABIC)

OPPOSITE

Dragon's blood trees growing along the rim of the Diksam Plateau, Socotra.

BELOW

The Indian cinnabar of legend: blood-red sap and crystals.

OVERLEAF

The Dragon's blood tree is marvellously adapted to its hot, dry native landscape on the island of Socotra.

Buyer beware: not all dragon's blood is what it seems. For more than two thousand years writers, explorers and scientists speculated on the origins and fabled properties of a remarkable garnet-red resin, so-called Indian cinnabar (the sulfide of mercury), said to be found on a remote and mysterious island.

In 1835 Lieutenant J. R. Wellstead of the East India Company first described the bizarre tree found on the island of Socotra in the Indian Ocean from which dragon's blood was, and always had been, carefully extracted by the inhabitants. Socotra has been geologically isolated for much of its history and boasts twenty-five endemic trees found almost nowhere else, including the only cucumber (*Dendrosicyos socotranus*) that grows into a tree and another that looks for all the world like a sack of potatoes (the desert rose *Adenium socotranum*). The true Dragon's blood tree grows on Socotra's semi-desert hillsides, resembling a magnificent but perverse giant mushroom or blown-out umbrella. Its trunk branches out from about 4 metres (13 ft) high into an inverted canopy of sky-probing limbs whose spiny leaves grow only at the tips of new shoots. When damaged, the bark oozes its famed red blood – a protective resin that can be tapped and collected, like latex. The tree is carefully protected on its native island and harvested sustainably.

When hardened into conveniently sized lumps, the resin is used medicinally as a cure-all, stimulant, muscle-relaxant and abortifacient. Other practical applications include a dye, an adhesive, a varnish for violins and a glaze for pottery, as well as incense in ceremonies and rituals. Scientists have isolated a large number of compounds from the resin, of which some have potential in treating cancers.[4] Other related species that produce chemically similar resins include the dragon tree of the Canaries (*Dracaena draco*), whose hollow trunks are used to fashion beehives, and the Mexican dragon's blood tree (*Croton lechleri*). Several other similarly coloured powders, including some derived from coral, are often sold under the name of dragon's blood. None, it seems, comes from the veins of a living, flying, fire-breathing beast.

Dark and light: the Pacific yew
Taxus brevifolia

LOCAL NAMES: YOL-KO (KONKOW FIRST NATION)

In 1962 the United States National Cancer Institute research programme was collecting bark from native trees, especially those known to indigenous tribes for their medicinal properties. Two toxic chemicals, called taxols, were obtained from the Pacific yew, native to the great temperate maritime forests that cloak the west coast of the United States from California to British Columbia. These yielded a pair of drugs – paclitaxel and docetaxel – that inhibit the multiplication of cancer cells, particularly in breast and ovarian cancers. Native tribes had long used the tiny leaves as a medical infusion, wound treatment and astringent bath. They also fashioned bows for hunting, boxes, canoes, utensils and fishing equipment from the yew's hard, dense heartwood.[5] But the Pacific yew, like its European counterpart *T. baccata* – of which almost all parts are very poisonous – is a relatively small and slow-growing, if long-lived tree. Harvesting the bark of several trees to treat a single patient created tensions between pharmaceutical companies and environmental campaigners. Synthesis of the two drugs has allowed the tree and its life-saving product to co-exist; and taxols are now considered a key weapon in the armoury of the oncologist.

Yews are remarkable plants in their own right. The multi-stemmed, large coniferous shrubs have thin, waxy, needle-like evergreen leaves and can live to an age of more than two thousand years. Because they do not always produce annual rings and because, in any case, mature trees rot from the inside and become hollow, it is notoriously difficult to date the planting of a single tree. By far the majority of ancient yews grow in the graveyards of churches in the British Isles, for reasons that are not entirely understood. The associations of the dark-green year-round foliage, a symbol of everlasting life and renewal, and the blood-red fleshy aril (which is, oddly enough, edible) that surrounds the hard seed, symbolizing sacrifice, made the yew an object of veneration for pagan and Christian alike. The European yews are famous for producing the longbow, its remarkable tensile strength and flexibility resulting from a combination of dark heartwood and light sapwood.

Arlington Heights Fruit Co.
Riverside
Riverside Co. Cal.

E. I. Schutt
Jan. 3 - 08
11 - '08.

Lemons and limes
Citrus medica; Citrus spp.

LOCAL NAMES: CITRUS (LATIN) TURUNJ, LIMU (PERSIAN);
ETROG (HEBREW)

OPPOSITE
A delicate but beautifully observed
watercolour of cultivated lemons by
Virginia-born US botanical illustrator
Ellen Isham Schutt, 1907.

OVERLEAF
Lemon trees in an orchard, Sorrento,
southern Italy.

Humans and their primate relatives, most bats, guinea pigs and some members of the sparrow family share an odd genetic flaw. Unlike the rest of the animal kingdom we have lost the ability to synthesize vitamin C, which is essential for health. Scurvy – a lack of ascorbic acid in the diet, causing lassitude, gum loss and the reopening of old wounds – was for centuries the scourge of sailors deprived of fresh vegetables and fruit. Consequently, Americans called British sailors 'Limeys' because they drank lime juice with their rum – a practice mandatory in the British Navy from 1796.

That link was first proven by Scottish doctor James Lind, in a brilliant maritime experiment on sailors in 1747 – although Lind himself was confused by the results (it didn't help that vitamin C was destroyed by both alcohol and the eighteenth-century distillation process used to preserve lime juice). Surprisingly, lemons are not the richest source of the vitamin, either (see Sea buckthorn, p. 93; rosehips are fifty times more potent; blackcurrants five times more so). However, lemons and limes – both long-cultivated hybrids, like the oranges, of a distant ancestor native to the Indian subcontinent – have long been used as a curative for all sorts of ailments, including heart disease and the common cold. In culinary terms, they balance sweetness and bitterness. The leaves are used as fragrant flavourings; the rind is grated and used in both sweet and savoury dishes; the soluble pectin in the rind makes an organic thickening agent, while citrus oil can be extracted for use in perfumery.

The citrus species are small trees or large shrubs with dark-green, shiny oval leaves, available in myriad varieties throughout the world and prized both for their fruit and as fragrant ornamentals. In 1907 two Norwegian bacteriologists, Axel Holst and Theodor Frølich, proved that the anti-scorbutic chemicals in lemons were water-soluble. By 1932 the Hungarian Albert Szent-Györgyi had isolated the vitamin – from a red pepper. The chemical structure was proven by the British chemist Norman Haworth in 1934 and vitamin C was first synthesized industrially in the same decade. In 1937 Haworth and Szent-Györgyi were awarded the Nobel prizes for, respectively, chemistry and medicine.

D.Blair F.L.S. ad sicc. del. et lith.　　CINCHONA OFFICINALIS, *Linn*.　　Hanhart imp.

Jesuit's bark: Cinchona tree
Cinchona officinalis; C.calisaya

LOCAL NAMES: QUINA; CASCARILLA; CARGUA

Physicians of Restoration England were understandably cautious about trying the papist-sounding Jesuit's bark on their Protestant patients. Apothecary Robert Tabor, however, who perhaps wisely formulated it as his own patent 'Wonderful secret', was knighted when he cured Charles II of what seems to have been a malarial fever. Tabor went on to dose Louis XIV of France and Luisa Maria, Queen of Spain, with similar success.[6]

A native of Andean forests, the cinchona tree and several sub-species attracted the attention of early European explorers because its bark was known as an effective medicine against malaria in humans and scrapie in sheep. Accounts of its first introduction to the Old World differ, but they go back as far as the early seventeenth century when Jesuit missionaries noted its use by the native Quechua people in the reduction of fever. Ironically, malaria was unknown in the Americas before the exploits of the Conquistadors. Quinine, the popular name for the alkaloid extracted from the powdered bark, became hugely significant in the treatment of fever caused by the infected bite of *culex* and *anopheles* mosquitoes, perhaps globally the greatest infectious threat to humans. Quinine is also a preventative, once widely prescribed for travellers to infected areas, and has virtues as a muscle relaxant. Bitter to the taste, quinine 'water' was frequently made more palatable with gin and lemon and has long since been associated with 'tonic'.

Cuttings and seeds taken from native trees have been cultivated across the Tropics. The bark is collected either from the trunk and limbs of a coppiced tree or by partially shaving two sides of the trunk without damaging the cambium layer beneath. Despite twentieth-century synthetic production of the drug and increased resistance to it by the malarial parasite, quinine remains both an important product and a subject of scientific study. A tree of modest size and appearance, the cinchona provides food for several butterfly and moth species. It is portrayed in Peru's official coat of arms. Pure native forms of the cinchona, growing at heights of up to 2,900m (9,500 ft) are at risk from deforestation and a decreasing indigenous awareness of its value and cultural history.[7]

The strangling Pipal
Ficus religiosa

LOCAL NAMES: PIPPALA (SANSKRIT); SACRED FIG; ARASA
MARAM (TAMIL)

In Buddhist sacred texts it is said that Siddhartha attained enlightenment beneath a pipal tree in Bodh Gaya in India, after forty-nine days of meditation. The pipal is a paradoxically aggressive companion for such gentle spirituality. It often begins life as an epiphyte, germinating in the crooked branches of other trees, then sending down aerial roots to the ground before, eventually, strangling its host. It is regarded as an invasive weed in many areas and its reproductive cycle, like other figs, involves the sacrifice of a partner wasp that pollinates its hidden flowers and dies in the process. But ancient specimens, said to be more than 1,500 years old, are greatly venerated not just by Buddhists but also by Hindus, and the tree is planted widely.

It is possible that the pipal's sacred significance was originally recognized by association with its medicinal virtues. Many tropical trees have reputations for curing all sorts of ailments from headaches and blindness to snakebites. In the case of the pipal it seems that many of these applications have a sound basis in science.[8] Infusions and oils extracted from the leaves have broad-spectrum antibacterial properties, and they are used as a topical aid in healing wounds. Extracts from the bark have been shown to be 100 per cent effective against some parasitic intestinal worms and to act as immunostimulants. Both fruit and bark exhibit antioxidant effects, useful in treating diabetes and atherosclerosis. An extract from the fruit acts as an anticonvulsant. All in all, the pipal makes for an impressive medicine cabinet.

Native to India as far north as the Himalayas and as far south and east as southern China and Thailand, pipals may eventually grow to more than 30 metres (98 ft) tall. The leaves are heart-shaped and a pale, luminous green. The fruits are smaller than the common fig (see p. 117) and not nearly so palatable. The massively long limbs create a cavernous, shaded canopy, often associated with temple buildings. Tannins in the bark are used in the leather tanning process, while bark fibres are processed to make paper. The light, soft wood is burned as fuel and made into packing cases and matchwood.

Laurineae.

Cinnamomum Camphora F. Nees et Eberm.

A whiff of chest-rub and gunpowder: the Camphor tree *Cinnamomum camphora*

LOCAL NAMES: CAMPHOR LAUREL; KUSUNOKI

Many extravagant claims have been made for the longevity of the magnificent camphor tree in its native Japan. There is no doubting the impressive size of some specimens, or its resilience. The venerable tree growing in the Sanno shrine in Nagasaki is the official emblem of a city that rose again after having survived the atomic bombing of 9 August 1945. The oldest individual camphor tree is said to be that at Kawago in Takeo City, on the island of Kyushu, measuring 25 metres (82 ft) tall and perhaps 3,000 years old.[9]

Across its natural range, from southeast China to Japan, camphor wood, roots, twigs and leaves have traditionally been steamed to release essential oils that have the unforgettable smell of mentholated chest-rub. The white crystalline substance produced by distillation of camphor wood is rich in volatile terpenes. Production of camphor became a major nineteenth- and early twentieth-century industry, the substance being used not just in medicine – as a local anaesthetic and decongestant – but also as an insect repellent, an alternative to mothballs, in smokeless gunpowder and celluloid film. By the beginning of the twentieth century it was a highly prized import to the West from Southeast Asia, costing some 50 cents per pound weight.[10] Concern over industrial monopolization eventually led to chemical synthesis of camphor from turpentine (itself distilled from pine-tree resin) in the 1930s.

In ancient Egypt liquid camphor was used as an embalming fluid; in medieval Arabic culture it was a perfume and cooking ingredient. But although camphor is still sometimes used as a flavouring in Indian cuisine, its culinary use is not recommended because of potential toxicity in high doses.

The evergreen shiny, waxy leaves are decorated by small, round, glossy black fruits. Owing to its attractive appearance, the camphor tree has been widely planted as an ornamental and introduction outside its natural range has seen it spread dramatically. In Australia and America the tree is considered a major invasive pest, competing with eucalyptus and, by releasing substances that impede growth (allelopathy), effectively suppressing ground flora.

SASSAFRAS

½ NATURAL SIZE

The rise and fall of the Sassafras
Sassafras albidum

LOCAL NAMES: WHITE SASSAFRAS; RED SASSAFRAS; KOMBU (CHOCTAW); WINAUK; PAUANE (TIMICUA)

Early European settlers exploring the botanical marvels of America's Atlantic coast were quick to embrace the supposed virtues of the sassafras, with its distinctive orange-vanilla-scented foliage, pyrotechnic autumn colours and leaves that look like the footprints of extinct megafauna. In 1571 the Spanish botanist Nicolás Monardes reported its many medicinal uses by indigenous tribes in his book *Joyful Newes out of the Newe Founde Worlde*. Sassafras root and bark were an apothecary's dream ticket, introduced to the English market by Sir Walter Raleigh in 1602 for their promised effectiveness against syphilis and becoming the second largest export from the colonies after tobacco. Four centuries later, scientific opinion has attached a large 'caution' label to the tree.[11]

The American sassafras is a deciduous tree growing up to 25 metres (80 ft) tall. Its dark, blueberry-coloured fruits are eaten and dispersed by birds, but the tree generates its own clones from root suckers, spreading rapidly in moist soils. The wood was once used in shipbuilding and furniture-making. Rich in natural oils, it also made good kindling. Roots, bark and leaves had a high reputation in native cultures for curing almost anything, from obesity to gonorrhoea. The twigs were also used as toothbrushes, dental anaesthetic and disinfectant. The root, which flavoured beers and was made into an infusion, is still a popular drink. Crushed sassafras leaves are an essential flavouring and thickening ingredient in the Cajun cuisine of the Mississippi Delta – especially gumbo sauce. All manner of syrups, cordials and tonics at one time contained sassafras oil but many claims were exaggerated and it fell from favour.

Scientific interest in the essential oils produced by the sassafras root led to the isolation of camphor, eugenol and asarone. When its main constituent, safrole, came under particular scrutiny, it was discovered to have a carcinogenic effect on laboratory rats in very high doses. In recent years, safrole's part in the synthesis of the 'party' drug MDMA (ecstasy) has attracted widespread public interest and concern and as a result, its extraction is heavily restricted.

Fashions, even in science, are fickle. The reputation of this fascinating and complex tree may rise again.

Neem
Azadirachta indica

LOCAL NAMES: INDIAN LILAC; NIMTREE; MKILIFI (SWAHILI);
THE VILLAGE PHARMACY (INDIA)

The neem tree is so useful in Africa, where it is naturalized, as well as in its native India, that it might fit in almost any section of this book. Leaves, flowers, seeds, wood, gum and bark are all valued – and in so many applications that it is hard to imagine traditional local communities functioning without it. Its protective and curative medicinal properties, central to Ayurvedic medicine and the practice of Buddhist ascetics, give it special cultural and biological significance; and, perhaps unsurprisingly, it plays a large part in celebrating religious festivals. The tree is said to be the dwelling place of many deities and is depicted in the early art of the Indus Valley.[12]

The neem is an evergreen tree, only shedding its willow-like pinnate leaves in drought conditions to limit water loss. It grows fast and tall, up to 40 metres (130 ft) and is widely planted alongside roads and in gardens for its shade. It produces both male and bisexual cream-coloured fragrant flowers on the same

ABOVE
On full show, the canopy of the neem dazzles like some geometric puzzle.

OPPOSITE
The dwelling place of many deities and provider of welcome shade.

tree and purple, olive-like fruits (drupes). The leaves are dried and used as an insecticide to protect clothes and dried rice, or infused to make a tea; both flowers and young shoots are eaten and added to various dishes as a flavouring.

Oil from the seeds, also an effective insect repellent, is thought to lower blood-sugar levels and to act as a detoxifier of blood, although in large doses it may be fatal. It contains the antibacterial agent nimbidin. Seed cake made from the pulp of the seeds is a valuable fertilizer. More widely, the oil is used in the manufacture of soap and medicinal shampoo and, when partly emulsified, as a lubricant grease. The bark contains tannin, used in curing leather, and also yields a coarse fibre. Resin exuded by the bark produces a glue, while the twigs make excellent toothbrushes. Combs are often made from the wood and are said to be effective in treating scalp conditions. The timber is termite-resistant and easy to carve. The neem's high reputation is well deserved.

1. Male and Female Branches of the Hippophae rhamnoides or Sea Buckthorn
2. to 10. different Species of the Hirudo or Leech.

London, Published as the act directs March 30. 181.

I.Pass.fᶜ.

Sea buckthorn
Hippophae rhamnoides

LOCAL NAMES: SANDTHORN; SEABERRY; SALLOWTHORN

OPPOSITE

The twigs, leaves and berries of sea buckthorn (accompanied by ten species of leech), in a coloured etching by J. Pass, c.1811.

BELOW

The orange berries of sea buckthorn were a crucial source of vitamin C through long winters.

The startling orange berries and long olive-green leaves of the sea buckthorn stand out against the matt yellow sand dunes of Europe's North Sea and Atlantic coasts and the tree grows along many rivers in central Europe and Asia. For the earliest hunter-gatherers and for traditional fishing communities, sea buckthorn was a nutritional lifeline through dark winter months. The small, sharply acid berries, which ripen and sweeten after the first frosts right into the cold season, are produced abundantly and are one of nature's richest sources of vitamin C, with ten times the equivalent of an orange or lemon (see p. 77). Had the seafarers of the world taken note of its traditional virtues in the great age of sail they might have carried enough to prevent scurvy long before sauerkraut or lime juice were routinely fed to sailors. As the *hippo* element in the Latin name suggests, the berries were also used in treating various equine disorders and to improve horses' condition.

Found in dry, salt-laden, high-altitude or mineral-impoverished soils, sea buckthorn – just like the leguminous shrubs of the tropics – thrives where few other trees grow, stabilizing and enriching the earth to which it clings. On these sunny, windswept sites it rarely reaches 6 metres (20 ft) in height, but grows in dense, impenetrable clumps. It is dioecious – separate male and female trees produce flowers, with the females bearing the fruit in autumn. Sharp thorns protect the trees from grazing animals, while coastal birds, especially thrushes, help to distribute and germinate the seeds. Sea buckthorn is often planted as a soil stabilizer, hedge and wind shelter. Leaves and bark yield a dark-brown or black dye.

Although the raw fruit is very sharp to the taste, it makes excellent preserves, juices and salad dressings. Ascorbic acid aside, the berries are rich in vitamins A, B1, B2, B6 and several minerals.[13] They possess antioxidant and antibacterial properties and yield an oil used in cosmetics. Scientists are increasingly interested in sea buckthorn's anti-carcinogenic potential and Asian medicinal lore as elsewhere places a high value on its properties.

From Apple to Walnut: the fruit and nut bearers

T HE FRUIT OF WILD TREES HAS BEEN COLLECTED, selected and cultivated for thousands of years, and a fruit tree lies at the heart of the Judaic and Christian creation story, the Garden of Eden. Along with nuts – which may, botanically, be either fruits or seeds – they are among the most commercially valuable crops in the world. They provide seasonal sugars, fibre, protein; a wide range of essential minerals for humans and animals in temperate regions and year-round bounty in the tropics. Most modern fruits bear little resemblance to their wild forebears; they have been manipulated with extraordinary skill and dedication by gardeners who have, wittingly or otherwise, used them to uncover some of nature's most precious genetic secrets.

Fruits and nuts are, so far as trees are concerned, devices for spreading their progeny at a distance. These nutritional offerings are a means of attracting birds and animals to take them away from the parent, germinate, deposit and fertilize them. This is no strategy: it is a mere evolutionary miracle (or a gift of the gods, if you wish to see it that way). Most trees bear fruit of one sort or another: the bean pods of the cacao or tamarind are fruits – that is, ripened ovaries from female flowers – as are hazelnuts, acorns and cherries. Some, like the mango, contain a single seed; others – the legumes, for example – carry many seeds in their pods.

Most humans consider fruits to be the fleshy sort – apples, oranges, pears and peaches – and nuts to be the hard seed kernels, yet for the tree, they are one and the same thing. What distinguishes fruit from nut trees in the wild is the likelihood that they will grow apart from others of their kind; they tend not to be gregarious, like oaks, beeches and hazelnuts, but there are many exceptions to the rule. Another way of looking at fruit trees is to divide them between those that give rise to offspring like the parent – often, again, these are 'nuts'; and others, like the apple. Trees in this second group need a pollinating partner and their propensity to scramble their genes in reproduction means that the most desirable varieties must be cloned by grafting – and some trees are harder

Harvested peaches ripening in
Cappadocia, central Turkey.

to graft than others. Some, like the peaches and sour cherries, are self-fertile, needing no partner at all. The most exotic of the trees in this section, or at least the most exclusive, must be the mangosteen; its narrow fruiting window and fussy climatic needs make it a rarity. Some other fussy trees became the subject of fashionable, not to say obsessive, cultivation in the walled gardens and heated glasshouses of the wealthy landed classes of seventeenth- and eighteenth-century Europe. The fleshy fruits have an aesthetic appeal like nothing else in nature.

A number of trees that might have sat very comfortably in this chapter have been listed elsewhere, because of their exceptional virtues in medicine or woodsmanship, for example. Several familiar orchard trees are included here; but also some less well-known fruits, including one favoured more by Australian emus than by humans. Each has a story to tell.

Several of the well-known and widely cultivated trees in this chapter have been fortunate enough to attract the attentions of the most exceptional botanical illustrators, including Deborah Griscom Passmore (1840–1911), Amanda Almira Newton (1860–1943) and Royal Charles Steadman (1875–1964). Because of the ludicrous prudery that prevented many women artists from gaining commercial success in figurative art and the propensity of genteel governesses to provide 'suitable' subjects for girls to draw, we have an outstanding legacy of female botanical artists whose acute observation and marvellous eye for colour would grace any art gallery.

Apple
Malus domestica; M. sieversii

LOCAL NAMES: POMMIER (FRENCH); ALMA (KAZAKHSTAN); MALUS (LATIN)

OPPOSITE

Branchlets, flowers, fruit, seeds and leaves of the European crab apple: after Hempel & Wilhelm, 1889.

OVERLEAF

Wild apple trees blossoming in the mountains of Kazakhstan.

If there ever was a Garden of Eden, it surely lay in the mountains of central Asia, where the apple, peach and almond originate. And if apples were the fruit of the tree of knowledge the original sin was, perhaps, to steal the secret of selecting, grafting and cultivating fruit trees – a feat generally credited to the armies of Alexander the Great (356–323 BCE).

Of more than 7,500 cultivars of the apple, almost all seem to be derived from a wild forebear, *Malus sieversii*. and Kazakhstan's capital, Almaty, is named after this once prolific and diverse fruit. Wild apples are individually so distinct because they reproduce heterozygously – the parental genes are mapped at random onto the chromosomes of the offspring – so a new apple might be unpalatably tart, with thick leathery skin, or a deliciously sweet new variety. Only grafting can reliably reproduce a selected and favoured characteristic. Most apple propagation is achieved by grafting a scion onto a rootstock of its hardy relative – a native of Britain, the crab apple (*M. sylvestris*).

The apple is a small deciduous tree, often growing to no more than 5 metres (17 ft) and most commonly seen in orchards where it is regularly pruned for shape and ease of fruit picking. Apple flowers are pollinated by insects, particularly red mason bees. The annual crop, harvested in autumn or winter, is vulnerable to late frosts. The rich diversity of known cultivars is considered to be at risk from both the decline of the bee population globally and from the neglect of older varieties whose diverse characteristics may be at odds with modern demands for pest resistance, shiny perfect skins and a uniform size.

Apples are usually classified as dessert or cooking, while specific varieties are also grown for fermentation into cider. The fruits are rich in vitamin C, carbohydrates and sugar, with some valuable trace minerals. They store well into winter and can be dried without significant loss of nutrients, hence their historic reputation as a soldier's marching food. The wood is close-grained and naturally self-lubricating. Although trees are not grown for their timber, it is used when available for axles and the toothed parts of mill gearing. When burned, the wood releases a sweet, rich odour.

Shagbark hickory
Carya ovata

LOCAL NAMES: PAWCOHICCORA; KISKITOMAS (ALGONQUIN);
POHICKORY

From Mexico in the south to Massachusetts in the north, the indigenous peoples of Mesoamerica and the eastern side of North America – whether Maya or Algonquin – possessed intimate knowledge of the qualities of the hickory from the shagbark of the north, the pecan of the south (*Carya illinoinensis*) and the pignut (*C. glabra*) to the shellbark (*C. laciniosa*) and mockernut (*C. tomentosa*). These closely related species are tall forest trees yielding superb nuts, timber of high tensile strength and a syrup extracted from the bark. Even so, it took the combined efforts of a freed Louisiana slave and a New York surgeon for these trees to achieve their commercial potential as nut-producers par excellence.

East of the Dakotas and north of Georgia, the shagbark is an unmistakeable icon of the forest, its immediately distinctive, self-shedding shaggy bark a key identifier. The leaves are compound, like those of the ash and walnut. The hickory soars high above other trees, often reaching more than 30 metres (100 ft), with the first lateral branches at over 25 metres (80 ft). The shagbark is slow to produce its first crop of nuts – perhaps after thirty years; but does so in abundance. Like walnuts, they develop inside a pithy fruit, the hard inner shell hiding the protein and vitamin-rich kernel. Nuts are knocked off the tree with poles and collected on large sheets before drying and shelling. The tree is monoecious – with separate male and female flowers on the same tree – and hybridizes readily, so that identifying the best commercial strains took the efforts of an enthusiast, Dr R. T. Morris. In 1905 he initiated a series of nut-finding contests that led to the best specimens being selected for grafting. But hickories do not readily graft, like orchard fruit trees. A former slave called Antoine had discovered the secret of grafting success in 1846–7 and his signature variety, 'Centenniel', is still regarded as one of the best pecans.[1]

The hickories are prized for the long, straight lengths of high-quality timber that – like ash – is used for spoked wheels, furniture, construction, tool handles and, not least, the traditional baseball bat. The several species of North and Central American hickories are a vital winter food source for many hibernating mammals.

The mighty Brazil nut
Bertholletia excelsa

LOCAL NAMES: PARA NUT; CREAM NUT; CASTANHA (BRAZIL)

In his classic 1948 book *Nuts: Their Production and Everyday Uses* the botanist F. N. Howes gave pride of place to the Brazil nut: the 'king of nuts'. It grows on a tall-canopied tree of the Amazon basin, with a single stem that branches out high up, perhaps above 30 metres (100 ft). The fruit, containing a dozen or so nuts, looks superficially like a coconut. Howes paints a fascinating picture of the nut trade in the immediate postwar period. The fruit ripens during the rainy season when, fortuitously, the rivers on which canoes or motor boats transported the nuts to market in Manaus or Itacoatiara were running full. At that time, when few commercial plantations were productive, collecting from forest trees was a hazardous business. Flooded rivers, primitive temporary camps, the inherent risks of climbing very tall trees, endemic disease and a diet of cassava were not the only hazards facing the nut collectors, or *castanheiros*.

'The collection of these fruits,' Howe writes, 'is not without risk to those engaged in the work and often fatal or serious accidents occur… These hard woody fruits weighing from 3 to 4 pounds and falling from a height of 100 feet or more strike the ground with considerable force. If one should happen to strike the head of a collector the dire consequences can well be imagined.'[2]

Because of its commercial value in producing nuts, *Bertholletia* is rarely felled for its hard and durable timber or for the inner bark, once used in the caulking of boat timbers; it now enjoys legal protection. But the outer casing of the fruit, the *ourico*, makes a useful cup or baler and is sometimes made into ornaments such as necklaces or bangles. The seeds, like acorns or hazelnuts, are buried in small caches by rodents, ensuring the natural means of forest propagation.

Their excellent flavour and high levels of natural minerals such as thiamine, Vitamin E, magnesium, phosphorous and selenium ensured the nuts' commercial value. They were first exported from Brazil and Bolivia during the 1830s. By the time that Howe was writing, some 30–40,000 tons were being produced for the international market every year. In 2014 it was about 95,000 tonnes. The nuts also yield an oil, locally valued for cooking and lighting.

Fragrant Pistachio
Pistacia vera

LOCAL NAMES: PISTAKION (ANCIENT GREEK); PESTEH (ANCIENT PERSIAN)

OPPOSITE
Ripening pistachio fruits.

BOTTOM
A pistachio orchard, Greece.

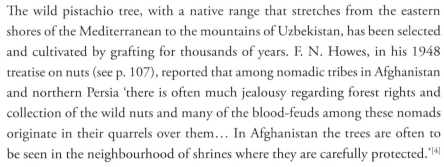

The wild pistachio tree, with a native range that stretches from the eastern shores of the Mediterranean to the mountains of Uzbekistan, has been selected and cultivated by grafting for thousands of years. F. N. Howes, in his 1948 treatise on nuts (see p. 107), reported that among nomadic tribes in Afghanistan and northern Persia 'there is often much jealousy regarding forest rights and collection of the wild nuts and many of the blood-feuds among these nomads originate in their quarrels over them… In Afghanistan the trees are often to be seen in the neighbourhood of shrines where they are carefully protected.'[4]

The fragrant pale-green pistachio nut (properly a seed) lends its distinctive, delicate flavour to the Middle Eastern baklava and Turkish delight, to Indian kulfi, and to Neapolitan ice cream. The very earliest humans to come out of Africa found wild pistachios growing in the Hula valley between the Golan Heights and the Sea of Galilee, along with wild almonds, acorns and water chestnuts, and relished their flavour and life-enhancing nourishment.[5]

Related to the cashew (*Anacardium occidentale*), the deciduous pistachio tree, growing to no more than 10 metres (33 ft) in height, enjoys the same climatic conditions as the olive and almond: hot, dry summers and cool winters. The blossoms appear before the leaves in spring and are vulnerable to frost. The tree is dioecious, with each specimen bearing either male or female flowers. It takes two years for the fruits to ripen, at which point the shells naturally split and can be collected – these days, generally, by machine. Sometimes male scions are grafted onto the branches of female trees to ensure local pollination.

The husk that contains the seeds, and wasp galls that grow on the leaves, are both valuable sources of tannins used in dyeing and in the preparation of leather. The seeds, rich in fatty oils and a range of key vitamins including thiamine, riboflavin, B5, B6, E and K, also contain calcium – they are perfect stores of winter minerals and protein. Those with a penchant for pistachios should be warned: stored in quantity in airless containers, the nuts have been known to spontaneously combust.

A gift of the Gods: the Pear
Pyrus communis

LOCAL NAMES: ARBOL DE PERA (SPANISH); POIRIER
(FRENCH); APIOS (ANCIENT GREEK); NASHI (JAPANESE)

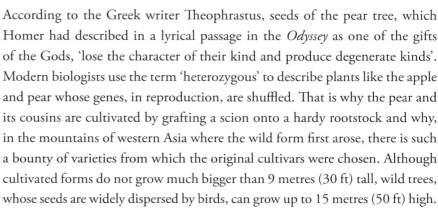

OPPOSITE

Vincent van Gogh, *Pear Tree in Blossom*,
1888.

BELOW

An unsigned watercolour of a cultivated
pear, from the Watercolor Collection of the
US Department of Agriculture.

According to the Greek writer Theophrastus, seeds of the pear tree, which Homer had described in a lyrical passage in the *Odyssey* as one of the gifts of the Gods, 'lose the character of their kind and produce degenerate kinds'. Modern biologists use the term 'heterozygous' to describe plants like the apple and pear whose genes, in reproduction, are shuffled. That is why the pear and its cousins are cultivated by grafting a scion onto a hardy rootstock and why, in the mountains of western Asia where the wild form first arose, there is such a bounty of varieties from which the original cultivars were chosen. Although cultivated forms do not grow much bigger than 9 metres (30 ft) tall, wild trees, whose seeds are widely dispersed by birds, can grow up to 15 metres (50 ft) high.

The pear seemed, to Europeans, such a lusciously decadent fruit that in many later medieval Bible illustrations the pear, rather than the apple, is portrayed as the forbidden fruit of the tree of knowledge – a temptation too far for the morally weak. For Shakespeare the withered pear was a pejorative metaphor; in France 'pear-headed' meant stupid; and 'pear-shaped' has its own negative connotations. But the fruit itself seems like an indulgent treat, a luxury.

The pear is now widely cultivated in all temperate regions in two main forms, European and Asian. The profuse white blossom, which appears in spring before the leaves, is a floral explosion against dark, bare hedgerows, and an early chance for pollinating insects to feed. The fruits are picked while unripe and, kept cool, will stay fresh. A cider-like fermented drink, perry (*poiré* in French), is made from special cultivars in France and England. Dried pear slices found in Swiss caves inhabited at the end of the last Ice Age show its value as a winter source of vitamins, and the ripe fruit, preserved in wine, syrup or honey is a feature of expensive cuisine.

The rich, dense, fine-grained, sometimes pinkish wood of the pear tree is used in cabinet-making, musical instruments (the 'jacks' that hold the plectrums in harpsichords, for instance), marquetry and inlay. Like the wood of other slow-growing fruit trees, pear is self-lubricating and was traditionally used to make the teeth of the gear cogs in wind-and water-powered mills.

D. G. Passmore
2.16.1904

Queen of fruits: Mangosteen
Garcinia mangostana

LOCAL NAMES: MANG-CHI-SHIH (CHINESE); MANGGIS (MALAY)

OPPOSITE

Mangosteen fruit and leaves, depicted in a watercolour by Deborah Griscom Passmore, a botanical illustrator for the US Department of Agriculture, 1904.

BELOW

Mangosteens on a market stall in the Philippines.

If the pear was once a synonym for luxury, it has since been displaced by the expensive, rare mangosteen. Almost exclusively grown in Southeast Asia, this delectable, exotic-looking fruit is harvested and sold only during a two-month annual window. In 2010 the first commercially grown consignment of Puerto Rican mangosteens, all 80 pounds of them, arrived in New York and were sold for about $45 a pound: $10 each.[3]

The flavour of the peeled, melt-in-the-mouth flesh is said to be a cross between a strawberry and a grape. Botanically a berry, the round, purple fruits grow on trees that may grow wild to 25 metres (82 ft) tall but which, when cultivated, are generally much smaller, with a broad, spreading habit. The mangosteen requires permanently moist, rich tropical soils, except for a short dry period that induces it to flower. It is commonly found by lakes and ponds or along stream and river banks. The tree is propagated from seedlings that are asexually produced by female plants, so that each of its progeny is identical to the parent. No grafting is required. It produces fruit after about eight years and can remain productive for over fifty years, yielding around 500 or more fruits at each harvest. Mangosteens are mainly grown on a local scale as a cash crop, by smallholders.

Each fruit, when peeled, reveals five to six kernels of white juicy pulp surrounding a single seed. The seeds are eaten boiled or roasted or added to flavour preserves. The rind is an astringent used to relieve symptoms of dysentery and diarrhoea, and to treat skin conditions like eczema. The dark wood is very heavy, quite durable, and used in construction as well as for furniture, tool handles or pounders.

Famed among travellers and gourmets from at least the fifteenth century, the mangosteen's fussiness for perfect growing conditions and legendary flavour ensure its continued scarcity on the world market and its precious reputation. For all humans' skill in bringing nature's finest produce to a global market, the mangosteen will, it seems, always be a byword for unattainable luxury.

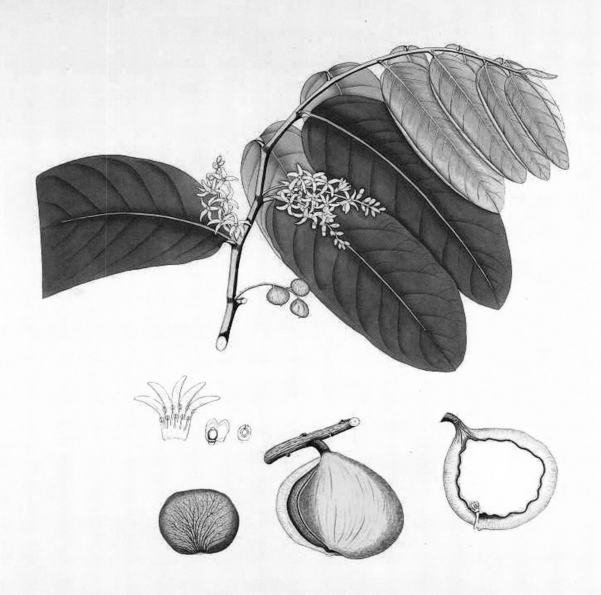

Swearpua edulis.

The prodigious Tahitian chestnut
Inocarpus fagifer

LOCAL NAMES: AILA (PAPUA NEW GUINEA); IFI (SAMOA, TONGA, HOORN ISLANDS)

Samoan folklore has it that the human race was born from the Tahitian chestnut. Although the *ifi*, as it is known in some of the Pacific islands, is worthy of inclusion here because of its highly regarded nuts, it has more than one string to its bow. From Java in the west to the Marquesas in the east, the *ifi* is found in warm, humid forests, gardens, coconut plantations, along riverbanks, in swamps and on coastal margins. Although it reminds Europeans of their more familiar chestnut, it is a legume – albeit one that does not seem to be as effective a fixer of atmospheric nitrogen as other members of that plant family (see Chapter 6).

Reaching a height of up to 20 metres (65 ft), the evergreen *ifi* flowers from November to December, with yellow-white fragrant blooms that bear fruit the following year, ripening from green to yellow. Each mature tree may produce an impressive 75 kilos of fruits each year.[6] The white seed that remains after the husk is removed is kidney-shaped, weighs up to 50 grams (2 oz), and is much loved by flying foxes and cockatoos. When boiled, roasted or grilled it tastes very like the sweet chestnut (see Chapter 4, p. 147) and is full of protein and carbohydrates. Crucially, the *ifi* is available at times when other staples like the yam are not productive.[7] It is eaten in cakes, breads and puddings or fermented for preservation. Uncooked, the kernels can be dried and stored as a food supplement.

The leaves, bark and roots of the Tahitian chestnut have a variety of traditional medicinal applications from the treatment of diarrhoea to burns and fractures, although the scientific evidence to support their use is limited. The large, waxy leaves are also used for thatching shelters. *Ifi* timber is used in furniture-making and for tool handles and canoe construction, while the wood is burned as a fuel. The *ifi* is also grown as a windbreak, a property boundary marker and as shade for crops like cocoa, sweet potato and maize. Its extensive lateral roots make it a good, wind-resistant soil stabilizer, especially for coastal dunes and riverbanks.

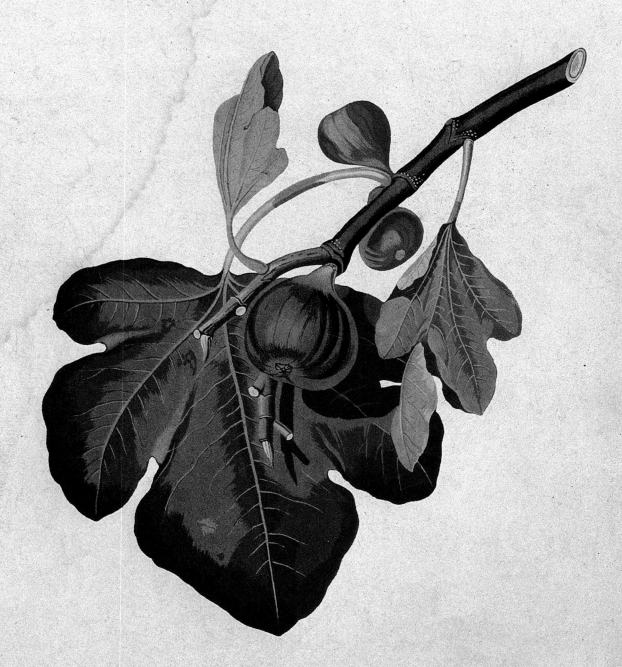

Ottavie Muzzi dis.   Gius. Pera incise

FICUS CARICA *Lusitaniensis*
Fico di Portogallo.

Nothing common about the common Fig
Ficus carica

LOCAL NAMES: ANJIR (PERSIAN); ANJEER (HINDI);
SIMAIYATTI (TAMIL)

In the New Testament parable of the barren fig,[8] an impatient owner exhorts his gardener to cut down a tree that has not borne fruit for three years. The gardener responds with a generous dollop of manure. Sweet fruits are greedy for nutrients: they cost their trees dear in energy resources.

The fig seems to pre-date even bread wheat as a cultivar, dating as far back as the tenth millennium BCE in its native Southeast Asian range. The distinctive large, lobed leaves are as instantly recognisable as the lush, sweet fruits eaten fresh or dried and stored. A relative of the mulberry, the fig is now widely cultivated around the world in Mediterranean-type climates and makes a fine ornamental garden tree growing up to 10 metres (33 ft) in height with a broad, spreading canopy offering shade from hot sun.

Looking for spring flowers on a fig is a waste of time: they grow, hidden from sight, inside the fruiting body as part of one of the most bizarre reproductive cycles anywhere in the natural world. As long ago as the fourth century BCE

Aristotle knew that a certain wasp that emanated from a wild fig pollinated the flowers and we now know that every species of fig has its own bespoke wasp for a pollinating partner. The female fig wasp bores a tiny hole into the immature fruiting body, lays her eggs inside – pollinating the flowers as she does so – and dies there. Her male progeny, as soon as they emerge inside the fruit, impregnate the still unborn females and then bore an exit hole, through which the egg-bearing females later emerge to seek their own new fruit. This self-perpetuating cycle seems to strain evolutionary credibility.

When the cultivated fig was first introduced to the apparently ideal climate of American Pacific coastal orchards in the 1880s, it bore no ripe fruit – notwithstanding attempts by gardeners to mimic the biblical parable and offer it more manure. Only when wild figs were imported along with their partner wasps did the experiment succeed. Modern 'parthenocarpic' cultivars have been developed that do not require external fertilization – good news for those fig-lovers who are squeamish about such things.

48925
"Royal Black"
amato Jassea
107 Penn ave n t.
Washington
D.C.

Elsie E. Lower.
10-12-'10
10-14-'10

38498
Peters No. 1
A. J. Pettigrew,
Manatee,
Manatee Co.
Fla.
7-18-07

J. A. Newton
7-26-07

The Inimitable Mango
Mangifera indica

LOCAL NAMES: MANGO (HINDI); MANNA (MALAY); MANGA (PORTUGUESE)

Most fruit trees are bushy – they put their energy into the fruit rather than trying to outgrow their competitors. Fruit cultivators like to keep their trees small too, to make harvesting and pruning easier. The mango, in its native India and Malaysia, is a huge exception, growing to more than 35 metres (115 ft). A genuine forest giant, it bears dark, evergreen, waxy leaves and heavy green fruits that ripen through yellow to a peachy flush. The mango tree, a relative of the cashew, may live and bear fruit for 300 years or more.

The wood is useful for all sorts of products, from furniture to packing cases and construction, as well as in the form of charcoal for smokeless cooking fires. The bark contains enough tannin for it to be stripped and used in leather-curing, and as a yellow dye. When cut, the bark exudes a gum used in the treatment of open-wound skin conditions; and even the flowers have medicinal benefits, in treating wasp stings and as an astringent to ease dysentery.

But it is the fruit of the mango that has generated hundreds of cultivars grown across the tropical world – most mango trees grown commercially being grafted to ensure the purity of the variety. It is one of the sweetest and juiciest of nature's gifts, prized as both a dessert fruit and, as an unripe ingredient, in curries, sauces and pickles. Unusually for such a large fruit, each one contains just a single seed. By the tenth century CE mangos were being grown in East Africa. Portuguese explorers brought the fruit back to excite and impress their royal courts in the fifteenth and sixteenth centuries. By the late seventeenth century, its virtues were being advertised by botanist-explorers in the treatise *Hortus malabaricus*, a comprehensive survey of the flora of the Malabar Coast of southwest India.[9]

Enthusiastic gardeners have tried their hand at growing mangos in Britain. For its first twenty years, the mango planted in the tropical glasshouse at Kew Gardens in the 1980s failed to produce. In the summer of 2009, however, after a winter during which the soil in which the tree was planted was inadvertently allowed to dry out, it finally and triumphantly bore two fruit.[10] The mango, as traditional growers know, needs a dry season to tempt it into production.

Wild cherry
Prunus avium

LOCAL NAMES: GEAN; SWEET CHERRY; MAZZARD

The pinkish-white blossom of the native sweet cherry – a relative of the plum – heralds spring in the towns and countryside of its native Europe and is an inspiration to artists everywhere. The shiny, emerald leaves, following soon after, are early to sprout, too. For such a common tree, there is much confusion between related species like the bird cherry (*Prunus padus*), which produces white candelabras of blossom but no edible fruit, and various cultivars. But there is no mistaking the bright-red or dark-purple fruit beloved of humans, birds and mammals.

Even in the depths of winter the dark, purplish-brown, shiny bark of the cherry stands out, pockmarked with the horizontal scabby lenticels through which it exchanges gases with the atmosphere. Its main shoot grows relentlessly upright and it is quick-growing, occasionally reaching the impressive height of around 30 metres (100 ft) or more.

Excavations of Bronze Age settlement sites in Britain (dating from between 2500 and 800 BCE) frequently yield ancient cherry pips, revealing the fruit to have been a British favourite for millennia. Cultivation and selection of the self-fertile tree has been traced at least as far back as the early first millennium BCE in Asia Minor, and many varieties are now grown commercially across the temperate world. Some of these are hybrids between the sweet cherry and the sour cherry (*P. cerasus*); the sharper the fruit, the more likely it is to be used for cooking rather than eating raw. The wild tree, its hermaphroditic flowers pollinated by bees, is propagated naturally by birds and mammals eating the fruit and distributing the pips elsewhere.

Cherries coppice readily and the dense, dark-brown wood is valued for its hardness and colour, for turning on a lathe, for cabinet-making and in the backs of musical instruments. Chips of the wood are popularly smoked to flavour and preserve meat, while the sap exuded from wounds in the bark makes a sweet natural chewing gum.

Cherries are widely planted as street trees and ornamentally in gardens for their early leaves and blossom displays. Oriental cherries (*Prunus pseudocerasus*), which have rather tart fruit, are famed and much celebrated across China and Japan in painting and poetry for their profuse blossom.

46949
Cerise de Montmorency
Mrs R. Smallwood
Linden, Prince Geo Co. Md
Montgomery Co.

D. G. Passmore
6.13. 1910
6. 17. " "

No. 64463

C. S. Pomeroy

South Glastonbury,
Conn.

E. J. Schutt
Sept 6 - 1913.
Sept. 8. 1913.

peach sport.

Peach tree
Prunus persica

LOCAL NAMES: PERSIAN APPLE; TÁO SHÙ (CHINESE)

Alexander the Great is said to have introduced the oriental peach, with its exuberant flowers and luscious fruit, to Europe in the fourth century BCE. If so, it would be a worthy legacy in its own right for the man whose armies conquered half of Asia before his thirtieth birthday. Peaches were already being domesticated in China and Japan in the fifth millennium BCE when European farmers were just learning to use a primitive plough to cultivate wheat. The peach tree and its fruit have attracted the devotion of artists and writers ever since. In China they are symbols of immortality, prized by gods and emperors and remaining popular as motifs in decorations and cooking. Murals featuring the peach can still be seen on the ruined walls of Roman villas in Herculaneum, beneath the dormant cone of Mount Vesuvius. Caravaggio, Rubens, van Gogh and Monet painted them and, more recently, David 'Mas' Masumoto's elegiac story *Epitaph for a Peach* [11] celebrated and mourned the decline of traditional peach orchards in America.

AMYGDALUS.

The Peach and Nectarine?

The Latin name, which reflects Roman belief that the peach originated in Persia, also betrays a common genetic origin with almonds, apricots, cherries and plums. Innumerable cultivars, including the smooth-skinned nectarine, are cultivated in warm, dry climates free of late-spring frosts. The tree will yield its first fruit after three years, but has a limited productive life span of about fifteen years. The UN calculates that in 2016 world peach production, dominated by China, reached 16 million tonnes. The pink blossom appears before the leaves in March, creating a spectacular floral show and offering early opportunities for pollinators to gather nectar. The lanceolate leaves are vulnerable to a fungal disease called leaf curl, especially in cool damp conditions.

Like all *prunus* species the bark can be dark-brown or purple and shiny, with horizontal eruptions – lenticels – similar to those on the birch and the wild cherry. The wood is slow-growing, dense and burns well, while wood chips from the peach are sold as an aromatic for cooking on open fires or barbecues. The peach stone, like its relatives the almond and apricot, has the distinctive taste of the chemical *amygdalin*, which releases cyanide, although not at remotely dangerous levels, when ingested by humans.

Desert quandong
Santalum acuminatum

LOCAL NAMES: DESERT PEACH; GUWANDHANG (WIRADJURI);
WOLGOL (NOONGAR); WANJANU (PITJANTJATJRA)

The Australian anthropologist and botanical illustrator Olive Pink (1884–1975) was no mere observer of natural and cultural history, but a fierce campaigner for the rights of indigenous Arrernet and Warlpiri communities in the Northern Territory. She was also the curator, with Johnny Jambijimba Yannarilyi, of a flora reserve on the Todd river in Alice Springs – now a public garden.[12] Her paintings of native Australian plants are infused with delicacy and a robust eye for colour and form.

The bright red fruit of the desert quandong is a favourite among the communities in which Pink spent most of her life. It is borne on an evergreen shrub, a relative of the sandalwoods, of very variable habit up to 6 metres (19 ft) tall with a domed or conical crown. The leaves are sharply pointed and conspicuously pale green. Remarkably, the quandong is partially parasitic, taking water and soil-bound minerals from host trees, especially nitrogen-fixing legumes such as acacia and casuarina.[13] Seed dormancy, and the need for a suitable host, make the quandong a difficult tree to propagate, but the increasingly popularity of its fruit has led to several recent attempts to cultivate it commercially. Its natural propagator and devotee is the emu. As a heat- and drought-tolerant native, the quandong grows across central and southern Australia, where it is an important food source not just to satiate the apetite of the emu, but for moths and beetles too. After bushfires the tree re-grows from its roots.

The fruit, high in vitamin C, contains a large nut whose surface convolutions make it look like a miniature brain. Separated from the fruit or collected from emu droppings, the nut has a high fat content and was once widely burned as a sort of candle. It can also be roasted and salted for consumption. The roots and wood, which have antibacterial properties, are a treatment for skin ailments, while the hard, heavy, close-grained wood is used for furniture-making and its twigs make handy fire-lighting friction sticks. The bark contains tannin. A collection of Olive Pink's botanical sketches is held in the library of the University of Tasmania.

Walnut
Juglans regia; J. nigra

LOCAL NAMES: ENGLISH OR PERSIAN WALNUT; NUX GALLICA
(LATIN); EASTERN BLACK WALNUT

Alongside the peach and apple and another native of Central Asia, the walnut is said to have been one of the prizes brought to Europe by the armies of Alexander the Great. In the mountains of Kyrgyzstan, great forests of pure walnut still cloak the land and their preference for exclusive occupation has a biological explanation. All the several walnut species (the black walnut, *Juglans nigra*, is native to the eastern half of North America) produce chemicals called hydrojuglones. Concentrated in leaves, roots, bark and leaves, these inhibit the development of ssss in many other plants (an effect known as allelopathy). As Pliny the Elder noted, in the first century CE, 'The shadow of walnut trees is poison...'

The walnut has always been prized: not just for its highly nutritious nuts rich in oils and especially B vitamins, but also for its strong, shock-resistant, beautifully figured dark-brown wood. This was used in gunstocks (12,000 walnut trees were felled in France in 1806 to provide musket stocks for Napoleon's Grande Armée),[14] fine furniture and in the dashboards of luxury cars, such

as Jaguars. A single tree that might sell for several thousand pounds would be converted into veneers of one-sixteenth of an inch thickness.

Walnuts are impressive trees in their own right: they can reach a height of 40 metres (130 ft), with a dense, spreading canopy. The leaves are a lush green and the drupes of green globular fruit, which contain the nuts, seem to weigh the whole edifice down in autumn. Walnuts are monoecious, with separate male and female flowers on the same tree. They are self-fertile and do not require a mating partner; and yet, they are adapted to hybridize with others, since the female flowers on any one tree emerge before the male (a process known as dichogamy). Most of the many cultivars grown commercially for nuts are propagated by grafting to ensure purity of a favoured nut – each one chosen for flavour, for ease of processing or for size and suitability on a particular site.

Walnuts respond well to human interaction: the traditional method of beating ripe fruits from their branches encourages the growth of fruiting spurs in the following year. A tree may be productive for several hundred years.

CHAPTER 4

Sugar and Spice:
a cook's bounty

Drying cacao beans on a farm in
Cameroon, Central Africa.

FOOD PREPARATION IS A SOCIAL AS MUCH AS A
nutritional activity, bringing families and communities together,
ceremonializing meals, celebrating the harvest of the seasons. It might
sometimes appear that the time taken to find, pick, peel, extract, wash, chop
and add raw ingredients to a meal is time wasted: Western supermarket shelves
are full of foods from across the world, ready to eat, prepared by unknown
hands for the sake of convenience. But collecting and processing are communal,
peaceable activities, times for storytelling and bonding between generations.
Many shells, skins, leaves and twigs that Western cooks might discard as waste
are used as food, fuel, animal fodder, for making toys or for wrapping and
storage; industrial processing is wasteful. And the careful preparation of raw
ingredients ensures that nutrients made available during the cooking process
are consumed as freshly as possible. Scientists now know that foods rich in fibre
– very often removed from highly processed foods – are essential for good gut
health and that, as a global society, we eat too few fresh fruits and vegetables.

Some of the most exotic ingredients, once the subject of wars between great
nations, are now generally and cheaply available and many cooks wouldn't know,
perhaps even care, where they came from. In this chapter the stories of some of
our most treasured culinary ingredients are collected together with the aim of
showing how connected these trees are, or were, to the communities that first
experimented with their possibilities. The journey takes us from the impossibly
remote Spice Islands (the Malaku Islands, or Moluccas, of eastern Indonesia)
that gave us nutmeg and mace to Andean cacao plantations and much more
familiar Mediterranean olive groves. Some of these trees have become symbols
of regional and national culture, central to ritual practice and indigenous art and
often playing key roles in wider land-use strategies involving grazing animals
and the growing of complementary crops. In one case, the extraordinary-looking
baobab, a single species can, literally, become the tree of life.

Many tree foods have medicinal properties: some are poisonous in large
doses; most are also grown for timber and shade, while extracts from leaves, bark

and fruits or nuts are used as infusions, for soaps, to treat wounds or provide lighting. Some of the trees included in this chapter end up in the kitchen cabinet primarily for flavouring and preserving traditional dishes – curries, soups, chutneys.

The champions among the culinary trees must surely be coffee and cacao; the former taken from just two of more than a hundred known species; the latter a former royal prerogative of the god-like kings of the Andes. Either is worthy of a book in its own right. Their stories reveal the best and worst sides of that restless desire to explore all that nature, and the world, has to offer; and, as the scientific analysis of their psychoactive properties advances, so they become more complex and marvellous. Cooking is, above all, chemical experimentation, an empirical search for the perfect partnership between humans and nature in taste, texture, smell and goodness. Separation from the earthy processes that connect people with the harvest of the trees leads to over-exploitation of monocultures like palm oil trees, or the monopolization of supplies that leads to subsistence farmers becoming disempowered cash-croppers. The wider the variety of tree foods that cooks and consumers enjoy and try, the broader the

collective aesthetic experience, with less reliance and pressure placed on land and communities to grow a narrow range of commercial crops.

In the temperate West, a very narrow range of foods is produced and consumed at commercial scales: a few grains; a smaller number of animals; a few dozen fruits and vegetables. Indigenous subsistence farmers and hunter–gatherers traditionally exploited a far greater palette of foods, many of them from the trees that they naturally found growing close to their settlements. Some of these are now commercially grown for just a single product, like cinnamon or almonds. But take a closer look at these trees and they all have other benefits for those who grow them in gardens, farm plots or on local hillsides.

Nutmeg and mace
Myristica fragrans

LOCAL NAMES: BUNGA PALA (INDONESIA); CHAN THET (THAI)

The Banda archipelago is a string of eleven tiny tropical volcanic islands lying southwest of Papua New Guinea. Now part of Indonesia, these are the original Spice Islands from which, until the late eighteenth century, all the world's nutmeg was exported.

The pale-brown kernel, which must be dried carefully for several weeks before it separates from its outer shell, is extracted by a swift whack from a truncheon. When grated, it yields the familiar, sweetly fragrant, rich reddish-brown powder used in baking and in flavouring sauces and meats. The extraordinary-looking fleshy red aril that surrounds the nut inside the ripening fruit is separated during processing. When flattened and dried it becomes mace, its own distinct aroma and flavour often used to add a spicy edge to stews and curries, or in sweet dishes as an alternative to nutmeg.

The Romans could sometimes obtain nutmeg from traders in contact with Central and East Asia. Later, Arab entrepreneurs controlled the supply through the Persian Gulf port of Basra, so that nutmeg prices were kept high in Europe while the virtues of the powder were exaggerated to mythical proportions.

The first Portuguese expedition reached the Banda Islands in 1512. A century later the Dutch East India company fought off both competition from Portugal and China and the resistance of the native traders to gain control of the nutmeg monopoly, before swapping its 'rights' with Britain for an insignificant American colonial possession called Manhattan. The suppression of the native Bandan peoples' autonomy and the appropriation of their wealth by the European powers is a tale of brutality and greed.

The nutmeg tree is of average height, growing to about 20 metres (65 ft). Now cultivated commercially well outside its home range, in China, the West Indies and across the Malaku Islands (Moluccas) of Indonesia, it bears dark-green waxy evergreen leaves. The fruit pulp is eaten before the aril and nut are processed. Both yield essential oils for use as condiments and in perfumery, while nutmeg butter is used as an ointment to treat rheumatism. While safe as a flavouring, nutmeg is a toxic psychoactive agent when consumed in large quantities.

Sweet Chestnut
Castanea sativa

LOCAL NAMES: SPANISH CHESTNUT; MARRON (FRENCH)

OPPOSITE
Flowering shoot, catkins, flowers, fruits
and seeds of the sweet chestnut: botanical
illustration after Hempel & Wilhelm, 1889.

BELOW
Ancient sweet chestnut tree, Croft Castle,
Herefordshire, England.

BOTTOM
Ripening chestnuts.

To appreciate the sweet chestnut in all its glory you must travel to the hilly forests of Corsica's Castagniccia (literally, 'chestnut country'). Here, thousands of acres of chestnuts, supposedly introduced by the Roman military and cultivated as a commercial crop by medieval Genoese colonialists, clothe the land in an emerald-green blanket punctuated by deep ravines and perched hilltop villages. Ripe chestnuts fatten the local pigs, are ground into flour to make bread and polenta or to flavour a unique local beer. The tree, its produce and habitat are synonymous with the regional culture.

The chestnut may originally have grown on the shores of the Black Sea. The Greeks seem to have introduced it to Italy. After that, wherever Roman armies conquered in the centuries either side of the birth of Christ, chestnut trees have been found – although there is some suspicion that widespread cultivation only began in the medieval period. In Anatolia, Italy, France, southern Switzerland, Spain, Portugal and Greece, the sweet chestnut is still commercially grown in either forests or orchards, where the nuts are harvested with rakes or by hand and gathered in nets. The chestnut coppices of Essex in southeast England, where the wood is still valued as a rot-free fencing material, may be a non-native legacy of the Roman legions.

Sweet chestnuts can live to well over 500 years, even longer if they are regularly coppiced. One famous specimen growing on the slopes of Mount Etna in Sicily is known as the 'hundred-horse chestnut', because its immense canopy is said to have sheltered a large party of the queen of Aragon's horsemen in a storm. The long, blade-like, serrated, translucent leaves of the chestnut are unmistakeable in spring. These are followed by pale-yellow spears of flowers and then by the prickly casings that protect shiny brown nuts. The pale fruit, after being roasted in its skin, is sweet and highly nutritious as well as gluten-free, low in fat, antioxidant and rich in vitamin C, minerals and starch. Many cultivars have been developed to enhance the size and flavour of the nuts, and it is a winter favourite for stuffing and puddings.

ACARUS, AND ACHRAS.

1. The Achras Sapota Plant. 2. The Cheese mite. 3. The Harvest Tick. 4. The Itch Insect.
5. The longicornis. or. horned Tick. all greatly Magnified.

London Published as the Act directs, Jan 30. 1808. by J. Wilkes.

Sweet Sapodilla
Manilkara zapota

OPPOSITE

A fruiting branch of a Sapodilla tree: coloured etching, *c.*1808, after Johann Eberhard Ihle.

BELOW

A sapodilla tree showing its waxy green leaves, Malaysia.

BOTTOM

Sapodilla fruit with burgeoning yellow buds.

The soft, ripe, juicy fruit of this evergreen native of Central America is said to taste of pears, cinnamon and brown sugar combined – no wonder it is highly prized by cooks for making jams, sherbets, custards and as a pie filling.[1] Sapodilla fruit is rarely found on the market stalls of Europe, however: unless perfectly ripe it is highly astringent, so the tree is difficult to grow commercially. Even so, it has been planted widely across the tropics outside its native range – in the Philippines, for example – because of its many other valuable properties and its tolerance of poor soils. The sapodilla grows to about 15 metres (25 ft) in height as a cultivated tree, but in the forest it can reach 30 metres (98 ft). The trunk grows long and straight and is deeply fissured, like an English elm. The leaves, which can be eaten raw or cooked when young, are a dark, waxy green, punctuated by small, white bell-shaped flowers. Their appearance precedes the development of the fruits, which look like small honeydew melons, no more than about 10 cm (3.9 in) in diameter, with a rough and firm skin. These are first produced when the tree is between five and eight years old. A mature, productive tree might yield 250 kilos (551 lb) of fruit per year.

Like rubber trees, the sapodilla exudes latex when the bark is wounded, and the trees have traditionally been tapped to collect it, both as a traditional chewing gum and as an alternative to gutta-percha. It is coagulated by heat and formed into blocks for export. The wood is tough, straight-grained and resistant to rot. It is used in heavy construction, in joinery and in making tool handles, but is not easy to work. The bark itself yields tannin, used as a curative for diarrhoea and for preserving ships' sails and fishing tackle.

Many other traditional medicines are derived from the Sapodilla. The leaves contain antioxidants and have been shown by experiment to counter diabetes and lower cholesterol. Pulverized roots are used to treat thrush. The shiny black seeds, like small beans, have antibacterial and diuretic properties; but they also contain hydrocyanic compounds, and are generally removed before eating.

1

5

2

3

Peint d'après nature par Mme Berthe Hoola van Nooten, à Batavia.　　　　Chromolith. par P. Depannemaeker, à Ledeberg-lez-Gand. (Belgique)

THEOBROMA CACAO.

Librairie C. Muquardt, éditeur, Bruxelles.

Drink of the gods: Cacao
Theobroma cacao

LOCAL NAMES: COCOA; KAKAW (MAYAN); CACAHUATL (NAHUATL)

The Kuna people of Panama, who drink natural cocoa in immoderate quantities, have low blood pressure, good renal function and display only a small risk of developing cardiovascular disease or type 2 diabetes.[2] No wonder the Aztec gods and god-like kings wanted the cacao tree all for themselves.

Little wonder, too, that Spain's conquistadors were not slow in bringing the first fruits of their violent tyranny to Europe, in 1528. In their natural state, the seeds of the extraordinary-looking cacao pod taste bitter; they must be fermented, dried and roasted, the nibs removed from their shells and then ground in to the aromatic, dark and bitter cocoa mass. Even so, the European palate demanded a sweeter treat – provided by that other colonial bounty, sugar cane. London's first chocolate house opened in 1657. The tree was transplanted to the Caribbean, where it formed a convenient partnership with sugar on British slave-owning estates, especially in Trinidad and Tobago.

Instantly recognizable when in fruit, with its giant pepper-like pods, the evergreen cacao shrub is unremarkable in size, growing no more than 8 metres (26 ft) in height. Its native range spans Central and South America, but it was probably being cultivated at least 5,000 years ago in lands that are now Peru and Ecuador. Its strong flavour, health benefits and psychoactive properties of lessening fatigue and improving brain function led to its adoption as an élite food, reflected in the Latin name *Theobroma* – drink of the gods. Mayan and Aztec mythology is rich in stories of gifts of cacao both to and from gods as part of elaborate and sometimes blood-curdling ceremonies. The beans were widely used as a currency, to pay tribute to overlords.

Three main varieties are cultivated: Forastero, Criollo and Trinitario. Trees are grown on both a large industrial scale and by small farmers, ensuring the genetic health of the tree. Climate change, however, seems likely to pose an increasing threat – and cacao is especially vulnerable because its seeds do not remain viable after freezing and drying. Modern production is dominated by Ghana and Ivory Coast in West Africa.

African Baobab
Adansonia digitata

LOCAL NAMES: UPSIDE-DOWN TREE; MONKEY-BREAD TREE;
ISIMUHU (ZULU); MOWANA (TSWANA)

Ibn Battuta, the intrepid fourteenth-century Arab traveller, was amazed by the sight of a weaver who had set up his loom inside the hollow trunk of a giant baobab tree in the West African kingdom of Mali. Africa's only native baobab – out of eight species, most of them endemic to Madagascar – has variously been used as water cistern, flushing toilet, prison and as a cool-beer store for a South African gold rush bar. It also served as a post office and bus shelter or temporary refuge. With its vast girth, five-pointed starburst leaves and immense age, it is widely regarded as having been planted upside-down by angry spirits.

But the baobab is, truly, a tree for food and for life. The leaves, rich in vitamin C, calcium and potassium, are eaten raw, cooked as a vegetable or dried as a thickening agent for soups and sauces; fresh shoots can be eaten like asparagus. The large seed pods ripen on the tree and contain a floury pulp that is either mixed with water to make a sherbet-like refreshing drink or kneaded into a dough for bread. The seeds are roasted and used as a coffee substitute, or crushed to release an oil used for cooking.[3] Bees make hives in the baobab's branches, so they are a famed source of honey for the daring climber. Bats seeking nectar pollinate the white flowers, which, in turn, are eaten greedily by passing animals and birds.

In severe drought conditions baobab trees can be tapped for water and the leaves become vital browsing fodder for livestock. The bark can be stripped to provide not just fibres for making ropes, nets and sacks but also a thirst-relieving chew. Like that of the cork oak, the bark re-grows after peeling.

Although baobabs rarely reach great heights, a tree with a girth of more than 10 metres (33 ft) may be 2,000 years old, rivalling the ancient yews of Europe. The baobab also yields a rich harvest of folklore. Drinking water in which its seeds have been soaked is said to ward off crocodile attacks, while an infusion of the bark is supposed to make a man virile. Spirits, thought to inhabit the flowers, are said to punish those who pick them. The baobab is one of Africa's natural and cultural gems.

A Serer cowherd harvesting baobab foliage
to feed his livestock, Senegal.

Indispensable Olive
Olea europaea

LOCAL NAMES: OLIVA (LATIN), ELAÍA (ANCIENT GREEK)

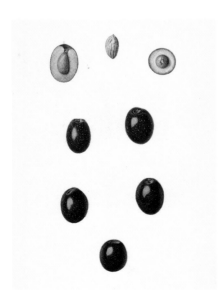

OPPOSITE

Vincent van Gogh, *Olive Trees with Yellow Sky and Sun*, 1889.

BELOW

A watercolour of olives (variety 'Manzanillo') by Royal Charles Steadman, a botanical illustrator for the US Department of Agriculture, 1917.

OVERLEAF

Olive trees in a grove on Crete.

The olive and its oil are indispensable in Mediterranean cooking, so much so that the tree and its pale-green fruit are emblematic of an entire culture, celebrated in every art form from Roman mosaics to the expressive brush of van Gogh. Humans have been writing about olives since the third millennium BCE, when they were already more highly prized than wine in the Middle East. On Knossos, the Minoan palace complex on Crete, clay tablets record early trade in olive oil.[4] Even Dark Age British chieftains and their Christian priests found ways to import precious supplies by boat from Byzantium. Highly localized and distinctive varieties of the tree have been developed over the last 6,000 years and the olive has been introduced wherever hot, dry growing conditions are found. Individual trees, small groves and hillsides planted with *Olea europea* on an industrial scale illustrate its ubiquity in the landscape. Olives rarely grow to more than 15 metres (49 ft) in height and display the characteristic dome shape suited to trees growing in lower latitudes. The evergreen leaves are shiny to limit water loss; their undersides a distinctive white or very pale green. Veteran trees, trunks and limbs, all gnarled and rheumy and polished by sheep and goats rubbing against them over the centuries, become architectural landmarks in their own right. Some may be as many as 2,000 years old.

The marvellous variety of tree shape, habit and fruit in olive cultivars is a feature, frustrating and exciting in equal measure, of its tendency to heterozygy: like the apple, its parental genes are randomly mapped onto the chromosomes of offspring, so olive trees grown from seed may be quite unlike either parent. Most are propagated by cuttings or layering.

The rich, pungently scented oil, traditionally released by crushing the fruit in stone mills before pressing the resulting paste, was once used for lamp oil and as a skin cleanser, but its huge commercial success has been as a culinary oil rich in unsaturated fats, high in calories and in vitamins E and K. It is a core component of the much-vaunted Mediterranean diet, said to prolong life and vigour. The fermented fruits are used fresh or cooked in a wide variety of dishes. The hard wood is prized by carvers for its density and richly coloured grain.

Nothing quite like the Tamarillo
Cyphomandra betacea

LOCAL NAMES: TOMATO TREE; TOMATE ANDIÑO; CAXLAN PIX (GUATEMALA)

OPPOSITE

A forgotten fruit of the Incas: the luscious tamarillo.

BELOW

Unripe tamarillo fruit on the tree, Jena Botanical Garden, Germany.

The tamarillo belongs, with the potato and the cacao bean, to the lost empire of the Incas. Growing high in the Andes, it was an essential component in the carefully engineered and managed terrace cultivation that these permaculture experts nurtured for hundreds of years before the Spanish conquest of the sixteenth century. It is a shallow-rooted, modest-looking shrub, a distant relative of the peppers, rarely growing to more than 6 metres (20 ft) tall and unlikely to live longer than twenty or so years. Both drought and waterlogging will put the tree under stress.

The tamarillo, propagated by seed or cuttings, becomes fertile after just one or two years, its fragrant pinkish-white hermaphrodite flowers soon attracting pollinating insects. Each shrub can yield scores of the luscious plum-like fruits, ranging in colour from yellow through to a bright cherry red, for a dozen or more years.

The ripe fruit is prepared by cutting it in half and scooping out the flesh. The flavour is variously described as like that of a piquant tomato, guava or apricot, with variations among the cultivars. It can be eaten raw, lightly sugared or, since it is high in pectin, made into preserves. In its native range the tamarillo is made into a popular salsa called *aji*, blended with chillies. It can be juiced or puréed, made into compotes or added to stews. The fruits, which are rich in vitamins A and C, in calcium, magnesium and iron, provide several important components in a subsistence diet.

Unsurprisingly, the virtues of the so-called tree tomato have been advertised across the subtropical regions of the world, and it is now widely cultivated from the southern slopes of the Himalayas to South Africa, Hawaii and New Zealand – where the name tamarillo was coined. Economic and scientific interest is focusing on the pest-resistant and nutritional properties of the tamarillo as an alternative to other, less reliable crops.[5] High levels of anthocyanins and antioxidants in the fruit suggest that it may have health benefits in subsistence communities where just a few trees add significant variety and nutrition to the local diet.

Aromatic Cinnamon
Cinnamomum verum; C. zeylanicum

LOCAL NAMES: KAYU MANIS (SRI LANKA); KANEEL (DUTCH)

Cinnamon is a member of the laurel family, related to both avocados and to the camphor tree (cinnamon root bark contains camphor; see p. 85). It has been a highly prized trading commodity for some 4,000 years, brought by seafaring traders from Southeast Asia to Egypt and the Middle East, from where its reputation as a luxury cooking ingredient spread to Greece and Rome.

During the medieval period, when exotica from the Far East were exciting the imaginations of the wealthy courts of Europe, Venice held a monopoly on cinnamon imports. During intense European competition for control of the spice trade from the sixteenth century onwards, British and Dutch traders began to exploit its commercial potential and expand cultivation of the tree in large-scale plantations.

Cinnamon is used to flavour savoury curries, pastries and festive wines. An essential oil can be extracted from the bark, and the berries and dried flowers are also used in cooking. Scientific analysis of the chemical composition of various parts of the tree reveals a complex suite of volatiles and oils.[6] These include eugenol, also present in nutmeg, basil, bay leaves and cloves, and cinnamaldehyde, which is extracted to flavour ice cream, chewing gum and some perfumes. Like many other tropical trees, the cinnamon is of interest to pharmaceutical firms: several folk remedies use the bark in treatments for inflammation and stomach troubles and as an antibiotic.

Of the several related species that yield the highly aromatic bark quills known as cinnamon sticks, *C. verum* is the most widely cultivated, particularly in Sri Lanka. A small, domed evergreen, it grows up to 10 metres (33 ft) tall with strikingly elegant boat-shaped, light-green leaves that show prominent, parallel cream-coloured veins. It is sustainably coppiced every two or three years. The outer bark is first scraped away then the inner bark is hammered to loosen it. The bark is prised off while still wet. On drying it curls up into familiar scrolls or 'quills' to produce one of the world's most distinctive spices.

St John's Bread

38302
"Ceratonia Siliqua"
P. J. Wester
Miami
Dade Co. Fla.

D. G. Passmore
mayth
May 20th
1907

A measure of gold: the Carob
Ceratonia siliqua

LOCAL NAMES: KARRUB; HARUV; ST JOHN'S BREAD;
LOCUST-TREE; GOAT'S HORN

OPPOSITE

Carob twigs, leaves and fruit: a watercolour
by the American botanical artist Deborah
Griscom Passmore, 1907.

BELOW

Gnarled trunk of a carob tree: Jezreel Valley,
Israel.

The carob is a multipurpose marvel of a tree: a pantry for the Mediterranean and Middle Eastern cook, a lumber store, a leguminous nitrogen-fixing soil improver, and a drought-tolerant evergreen hedge for smallholders and gardeners.

The otherwise humble-looking carob seed occupies a unique historical niche. It was once so widely recognized around the Mediterranean basin and so consistent in size that it was traditionally used by gold merchants as a measure of weight. Twenty-four carob seeds came to be the standard weight of the Roman gold coin known as the *solidus* – and hence 24-carobs (or carats) became a measure of 100 per cent pure gold and of proverbial quality. The carat is now standardized at 0.2 grams of pure gold; 12-carat gold is 50 per cent pure.

The carob tree grows to about the same size and shape as an olive tree, with which it shares much of its geographical distribution. The unmistakeable shiny dark-brown pods ripen once a year on either female or hermaphrodite trees. The carob becomes productive after eight to ten years and matures at around twenty-five years. It is generally resistant to pests and, like other leguminous plants, may also help to improve soils by fixing atmospheric nitrogen in its extensive root system.

Widely cultivated for at least 4,000 years and propagated from seeds, the carob is grown largely for its pods, which take a year to ripen. They are knocked off their branches with long sticks during a single annual harvesting period while the tree is still in flower. The pods are dried and the precious pulp removed, powdered and added to food as a flavouring or made into a sweet syrup. With a taste not unlike chocolate, it is often used as a substitute, free from both caffeine and the theobromine that is harmful to some mammals. The pod meal makes a nutrition-rich animal fodder containing proteins, starch and glucose and several important vitamins, but very little fat.[7] A gum produced from the crushed and roasted seeds is used as a thickening agent, gluten substitute and ice-cream stabilizer. The wood is hard and dense, burns well as a domestic fuel and can be used for ornamental carving and furniture.

36163
Avocado
Mrs. P. H. Rolfs
Miami
Dade Co. Fla.
7-2-'06

A. A. Newton
7-3-'06

Avocado
Persea americana

LOCAL NAMES: AHUACAQUAHUITL (NAHUATL); AGUACATE (SPANISH); ALLIGATOR PEAR TREE

Ethnobotanists are fascinated by the origins of useful plants whose domestication is lost in the mists of time. They use the term 'cultigen' for trees like the avocado, a probable native of Mexico's Tehuacán valley, which has been cultivated for several thousand years and formed part of the diet of pre-Aztec peoples. A fossilized avocado pip from deposits in Coxcatlan Cave dates from 9,000 to 10,000 years ago, while a very old, semi-wild form of the avocado, known as criolla, is still grown in Central and South America. In regions where the avocado is a commercially valuable tree – especially Mexico, Guatemala and California – varieties are selected for both flavour and to suit local climate and soil conditions.

The creamy, buttery-sweet flesh of the unpronounceable *ahuacaquahuitl* ensured its spread throughout the pre-Columbian Aztec, Maya and Inca empires, wherever consistently warm and wind-free conditions were available for its cultivation. Spanish explorers were writing home about it in the early sixteenth century, and the Anglicized term 'avocado' was first coined by the naturalist and collector Hans Sloane in a 1696 catalogue of Jamaican plants.[8]

The avocado may grow to a surprising height – up to 20 metres (66 ft), with characteristic waxy ovate evergreen leaves and unmistakeable reptilian-looking dark-green fruits. It can be grown from seed, as every school pupil knows; but to ensure consistent size, quality and quantity in commercial plantations, the avocado is usually grafted onto a hardy rootstock.

The fruit, which ripens after picking, is eaten all over the world in ever-larger quantities. A staple of Mexican cuisine, where it is eaten fresh as a salad (alongside the aniseed-like leaves), or as a guacamole dip, it can be found in both savoury and sweet dishes. It contains very high fat levels, important in vegetarian and vegan diets, and is rich in minerals and vitamins A, D and E.[9] Avocado oil obtained from both pulp and seeds contains phytosterols, which give it a high smoke-point, while it is also an ingredient in soap and skin lotion manufacture. The timber from felled trees is valued for furniture-making and decorative carving.

Indian curry-leaf tree
Murraya koenigii

LOCAL NAMES: SWEET NEEM; KARRI PATTHA (INDIA, SRI LANKA)

No bigger than a small but densely green shrub, the pretty curry-leaf tree, a relative of the citrus, exudes a smell instantly and uniquely redolent of southern Indian and Sri Lankan cooking. Yet it is also valued elsewhere in Southeast Asia and as far north as Nepal. The complex chemistry of the leaves, so essential to its fragrance and the flavour it imparts to food, derives from essential oils that include sabinene (also present in black pepper, Norway spruce and nutmeg), caryophyllene (found in cloves and basil), and cadinene, a source of aromatic cade oil (first found in a type of juniper).

Curry leaves can be used fresh, dried or powdered (the curry powder found in shops, is, confusingly, not powdered curry leaves but a mixture of several spices). The curry leaf in Indian cooking is like the bay leaf in the Mediterranean: a universal in the spice cabinets of every kitchen and restaurant. Dhals, Madras curries and mulligatawny soup are among its most common uses. Leaves – a whole stalk's worth, but without the stalk – are bruised and sometimes sautéed in oil before the addition of other ingredients.

Flavouring aside, the leaves contain vitamins A, B2, C and important traces of iron, zinc, calcium and copper. They have been shown to produce a stabilizing effect on blood glucose levels and claims have been made for their efficacy in the successful treatment of diabetes.[10] Green leaves are eaten to combat the effects of dysentery and nausea, especially in response to morning sickness during pregnancy. Oil extracted from the leaves is used in soap-making.

The bark and roots of the curry leaf tree are used in the treatment of skin conditions and poisonous bites. The dark-red or black fruit can also be eaten: it has a peppery taste and, when pulped and mixed with lime juice, is used to soothe insect bites.

The foliage, fragrant white flower clusters and berries make the curry-leaf tree an attractive ornamental for small gardens. It is easy to propagate from suckers, but this means that it can be invasive if not controlled.

Plate V.

COFFEA *Arabica*

A   *S. Taylor Pinx!*   B   C   D   F   G   H   E   *J. Miller Sc*

Coffee
Coffea arabica; C. canephora/robusta

LOCAL NAMES: BUNA (ETHIOPIA)

OPPOSITE

The flowering and fruiting stem of *Coffea arabica*: a coloured engraving by J. Miller, *c.*1774, after S. Taylor.

BELOW

Coffee berries ripening on the tree.

OVERLEAF

A coffee plantation at sunset, Colombia.

Nature has provided the world with 124 species of coffee, a small bush with red berries native to Africa and Asia. Between 2016 and 2017 humans consumed more than 150,000 60-kilogram bags of the stuff [11] from just two species. Both originate in the mountain rainforests of Ethiopia and both are cultivated across the tropical world. The first credibly recorded consumption of the bean – properly the seed – comes from fifteenth-century Yemen, when Sufi worshippers drank it to maintain alertness during long religious ceremonies. Europe's first coffee house was opened in Rome in 1645; Oxford's Queen's Lane Coffee House has been open since 1654. Like several others among the cultivated trees in this book, coffee played its own ignominious part in the colonial slave trade in the Americas.

Scientists are increasingly concerned that the rich genetic diversity of the other 122 species, in which, for example, caffeine-free and self-fertile genes are found, is in danger of being lost, leaving the world heavily reliant on its two favoured cultivars. [12] In the face of potential plant disease, pest attack and climate change, the coffee bush is vulnerable. If the richness of diversity among the trees in this book is a guide, the risks of losing species before their potential has been understood ought to be obvious. *Coffea robusta*, whose beans produce 40 per cent of the world's blended coffees, and which is mostly cultivated in Vietnam, was only discovered in 1897, bringing pest resistance and a high yield to the genetic pool. The wild genes still out there may offer equal riches.

The coffee bush, often grown as a crop alongside others to provide shade and among fruit and vegetable plots, is propagated from seeds that normally come in pairs inside each berry. Berries must be picked at the right time for perfect results, so they are generally still harvested by hand, mechanically stripped of their flesh, then dried – or wet-fermented and dried – before being roasted at precise temperatures for precise times to caramelize and release their starches as sugar. As all consumers know, caffeine in the resulting drink, coffee, is both a stimulant and appetite suppressor; but coffee is more than just caffeine.

Sugar maple
Acer saccharum

LOCAL NAMES: ROCK MAPLE

The North American sugar maple is a show-off of a tree, breathtakingly exuberant in its dazzling autumn splendour and celebrated for its extraordinary ability – one of nature's closely guarded secrets – to survive the effects of severe freezing.

A tall (up to 45 metres/148 ft), long-lived tree of cool and temperate forests, and a relative of the sycamore (*Acer pseudoplatanus*) and field maple (*A. campestre*), the sugar maple dominates extensive forests on both sides of the US–Canada border. Its distinctive five-pointed, lobed leaf is the emblem of Canada. The leaf shape, and its pairs of 'helicopter' winged seeds, are a characteristic shared with the other maples.

As a timber tree the sugar maple produces whitish, cream or pink straight-grained, easily split and worked timber, sometimes with attractive figuring, used in flooring and furniture; its lightweight and resonant properties make the wood ideal for the soundboards of violins and guitars and the shells of drums.

The key to its autumn colours and its winter survival is sugar. In autumn, sugars and minerals are being recycled from leaves into storage in the vessels of the trunk. A range of brightly coloured chemicals such as anthocyanins and carotenes are left behind as green chlorophyll is lost, until the leaf is discarded. In very hard frosts the water columns of trees freeze and the spring thaw leaves air cavities behind which can break the suction/adhesion effect by which water is drawn up to the leaves. This is potentially fatal. Maples, along with the cold-adapted birches, are able to generate a positive internal pressure in their roots – no one is quite sure how – pumping a sugary sap up the water column to force out air cavities and restore transpiration. The thickness of the sugar solution is one part of the answer; a side effect is the build-up of sugary sap with a pressure much higher than that of the external atmosphere. Any damage to the bark, or a carefully controlled tapping hole drilled into the phloem, releases the sap, which is collected like latex and boiled to produce the famously sweet and fragrant reddish-brown syrup. Forty gallons (180 l) of sap make one of syrup. It is a favourite ingredient in desserts and one of America's signature dishes, the sweet pancake. Maple syrup is also tapped from the black (*Acer nigrum*) and red maples (*Acer rubrum*).

A painter's tree: Almond
Prunus dulcis

LOCAL NAMES: GREEK NUTS; ALMENDRA (SPANISH); AMANDE (FRENCH)

OPPOSITE

Spring almond blossom, Andalucía, southern Spain.

BELOW

Shelled almonds, ready for market.

The blossom of an almond tree is a sight to lift the spirits at winter's end. In California, in February, hundreds of thousands of beehives are brought to the almond groves for a mass pollination. The trees seem to vibrate in perfect pink harmony. Painters like Vincent van Gogh have found them irresistible subjects.

The almond is no American native but was introduced, like the apple and walnut (see Chapter 3) from Central and Southwest Asia. Its wild forebear *Amygdalus communis* is a dry-soil mountain dweller.[13] By the middle of the second millennium BCE the virtues of domesticated almond cultivars were known in the Mediterranean – among the presents said to have been taken to Egypt by the sons of Jacob in the Book of Genesis. Two main varieties, bitter and sweet, have given rise to innumerable local cultivars of major economic value.

Where its close relative, the peach, bears a soft, fleshy and sweet fruit, the almond's is dry and leathery. But the peach stone is inedible, whereas the almond is a culinary gem. While still unripe the kernels can be removed from the fruit and shell and preserved in sugar as a sweet treat. Ripe almonds are eaten raw. Blanched, they are ground into a paste with sugar or honey to make marzipan for cakes and frangipani for tarts, and flavour many well-known biscuits and desserts. In India they are a key ingredient in passanda sauces. Almond butter makes a luxurious alternative to peanut butter and almonds are used to flavour liqueurs such as Italian amaretto. A milk exuded from the crushed seeds is a popular alternative to cow's milk and soya milk in a vegan diet. The oil is very fine and used in technical engineering applications such as sewing machines. Almonds are high in carbohydrates, monounsaturated oils and protein, with naturally high levels of vitamins B2 and B3 and the minerals manganese, magnesium, phosphorus, calcium, copper and iron – a rich nutritional package to support healthy diets.[14]

Almond trees may grow up to about 10 metres (33 ft) in height; they bear nuts from about their fourth year, gradually increasing production over another twelve to twenty years.[15]

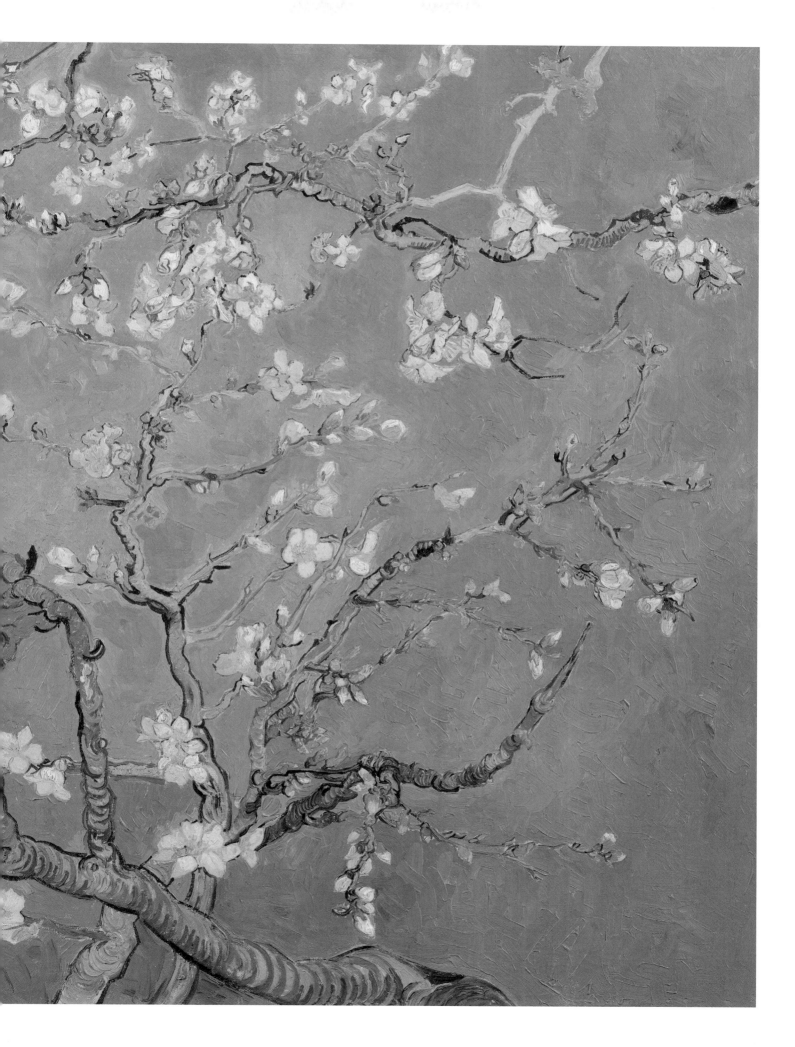

CHAPTER 5

Supertrees

WHAT MAKES A TREE A SUPERTREE? THIS IS A personal selection – there is no definitive answer. But, from the lordly Scots pine to the tropical coconut and the goat-bearing argan, these are all multitasking trees with a rich cultural history; each one plays a pivotal role in maintaining natural and social communities. The Scots pine and the oak form vast climax woodlands across the Eurasian land mass. Invaluable timber species with highly complex ecologies, they also attract rich mythologies and admiring artists; they are superbly useful and much loved. More than that, they have a significant landscape impact as both single trees and forests; they are genetically and behaviourally diverse and supportive of large communities of insects and birds.

Supertrees express much of the diversity that 300 million years of evolution and sexual reproduction have generated and they reinforce our wonder that such variety of shape, size, material, habit and usefulness can come out of apparently simple components like water, carbon dioxide, sunlight and a few trace minerals. The ingenuity of human exploitation is celebrated here too – from the challenge of picking a coconut from thirty metres above ground to transporting breadfruit seedlings from one hemisphere to the other in a wooden sailing ship with a problematic crew. On the other hand, our drive to explore and exploit these trees risks constricting global biological diversity, even the extinction of many ancient species. Nature's jury is casting a cold eye on the human propensity to test its environment to destruction.

Some of the trees included here attract controversy because while, for some, they are miraculous life-givers, to others they offer false hope of tackling global environmental crises in land-management and carbon-capture. Several are best known for their large, showy and valuable fruits, but bring much more to the party: both the record-breaking jackfruit and the elegant date palm are surprisingly versatile and generous with their gifts. Others have played significant bit parts in our history – like Pacific breadfruit, as valuable for its wood as for its floury edible pulp, which became embroiled in a scandalous and

riveting saga of mutiny aboard the *Bounty* in 1789. A vignette of the coconut appears in the tales of the *Arabian Nights*, while the coolibah tree became a legendary touchstone for the presence of gold in the Australian outback and the Buddha is said to have died in the shade of two sal trees. One or two of these supertrees are well-kept secrets, neither showy nor much celebrated outside the communities who value them. The kou, that oceanic Argonaut, and the mulga acacia are barely more than shrubs, but highly adapted, highly productive and invaluable as social and economic assets. The argan, a crucial and protected marvel of Morocco's vulnerable Atlantic plain, seems to bear the strangest fruit of any species and reminds us that humans are not the only creatures who feel a strong affinity with trees.

Above all, these supertrees encapsulate the dynamic, often affectionate, sometimes overwhelmingly pragmatic relations between trees and human communities across the world. Such rich cultural partnerships, some of which are so ancient as to be obscure in their origins, have given rise to a specific term, 'cultigen', coined by ethnobotanists to describe trees that were domesticated or cultivated before human history was able to record them. They are symbolic of both an enduring partnership and of hope for our future role as global guardians.

Lordly oaks
Quercus robur; Q.petraea and spp.

LOCAL NAMES: ENGLISH OAK; CHÊNE (FRENCH); ROBLE (SPANISH)

OPPOSITE

Branchlets, leaves, flowers and acorns of the pendunculate oak: botanical illustration after Hempel & Wilhelm, 1889.

BELOW

A veteran oak in grassland, Glenridding, Cumbria, in England's Lake District.

The oak is a dominant forest tree of the northern hemisphere, an ecosystem all of its own and a keystone species for a wide variety of habitats. It is the tree of proverbial national strength and character. There are more than 600 oak species, with the richest variety found in China, Mexico and North America. In Europe the deciduous *Quercus robur* (English or pedunculate oak) and *Q. petraea* (sessile oak) reign supreme, but cork oaks (*Q. suber*: see Chapter 1, p. 45) and holm oaks (*Q. ilex*) sometimes form evergreen forests further south in Mediterranean climates.

Oaks grow to a great age and size – specimens of over 1,000 years old can be found in countries across Europe. They support large numbers of insects and birds, form partnerships with other trees and ground flora and are known to communicate using chemical warning signals: they release vaporized tannin into the air during severe insect infestations. The timber is highly valued for its great strength and resilience. Traditionally it was felled and sawn or split while still green; seasoning was completed within the structure of a building

and the wood became harder with age. Palaces, halls and ships of great size and sophistication relied heavily on oak for their construction. Oak barrels used in fermenting wine, whisky and beer spawned a large, widespread coopering industry from the medieval period. Wasp galls forming on oak twigs were processed to make a permanent black ink used in manuscripts like the Lindisfarne Gospels. Oaks were often allowed to mature to ages of between 100 and 150 years to produce fine timber; but large areas of oak woodland came under coppice management to allow regular cropping, every twenty years or so, of oak poles for construction. Many place names including the Old English element *Ac-* reflect once-prominent individual trees or woods. It is hard to imagine our landscapes without them.

Acorns, usually collected by birds – especially jays – are buried in large numbers every autumn and germinate readily, although there is concern about a decline in oak re-growth in some areas. Acorns, like beech nuts, were traditionally browsed by pigs to fatten them for winter slaughter. Most are unpalatable to humans unless washed clean of their toxins, although the holm oak yields edible acorns. Oak bark is very highly prized for its rich tannins, used in curing leather. Oaks are genetically diverse and hybridize readily; even so, a number of diseases and pests, notably Acute Oak Decline (AOD) in the UK, threaten populations in many areas.

An oceanic Argonaut: the Kou
Cordia subcordata

LOCAL NAMES: KEROSENE; SEA TRUMPET; ISLAND WALNUT; NAWANAWA (FIJIAN); KALIMASADA (JAVANESE)

OPPOSITE

Twigs, leaves, flowers and fruit of the kou tree, in a watercolour by Sydney Parkinson made during Captain Cook's first voyage across the Pacific, 1768–71.

BELOW

The bright orange kou flower, Oahu, Hawaii.

The versatile wood of the kou is well known to the craftspeople of coastal Asia, Africa, Australia, the Indian Ocean and the Pacific islands. As its distribution suggests, the sea is also its means of propagation; the buoyant seeds are able to germinate after drifting thousands of miles on ocean currents.

The light wood, with a purplish tinge and odd black streaks, is easily worked for all sorts of domestic construction purposes from furniture to beams and posts, musical instruments, canoes and paddles. Carved to make containers and utensils, it does not taint food. Boxes, ornaments and souvenirs, which can be polished to a fine lustre, are highly valued, providing a sustainable source of income in coastal settlements, especially those with a thriving tourist industry. Kou wood burns so readily that fires can be started by rubbing two sticks together. The inner bark yields a fibre used in making baskets and skirts, hats and fans.[1]

The kou is a small, fast-growing genetically diverse shrub with dense foliage, rarely growing to more than 10 metres (33 ft) tall. On account of its low-hanging branches and attractive orange flowers, it is popularly grown as a windbreak and living fence. Salt-tolerant, its value in coastal protection schemes is increasingly appreciated, and it has been shown to detoxify soils contaminated with petrochemicals.

The fragrant orange flowers of the kou are often seen in *lei*, or floral garlands, traditionally given as gifts in the Hawaiian Islands. The leaves and bark yield a brown or reddish dye and are consumed as fodder by domestic pigs. The seeds, produced abundantly, are said to be edible in times of famine – which does not say much for their flavour. Around the Pacific Rim, the tree is regarded as having sacred value as a clan totem. Oddly, the kou is little used or valued in tropical Africa where it might be expected to be cultivated; agroforesters suggest that it may have a value in intercropping and as a pioneer species but warn that overexploitation may lead to its local disappearance.[2]

Eating Dates

Feeding Cattle on Date stones.

Palm Sunday

Drinking Arrack.

Mats and Baskets of Palm leaves.

Embryo

Date opened.

Date.

Using Palm wood.

The date palm
Phoenix dactylifera

LOCAL NAMES: MEDJOOL (MOROCCO); DEGLET NOOR (ALGERIA); ABID RAHIM (SUDAN)

OPPOSITE
The myriad uses of the date palm as depicted in a coloured lithograph, *c*.1840.

BELOW
A Canary Island date palm ornaments the gardens of San Giuliano near Catania, Sicily.

OVERLEAF
Date palms fringe the oasis at Um el Ma in the Libyan Sahara.

In any street market in Egypt, Iran or Algeria and across the Arab and Mediterranean world you will find dates in all their luscious variety, ready to eat or to be cooked in sweet dishes. No Middle Eastern scene is complete without the tall, columnar palm stems and a firework burst of green fronds rippling in a hot desert breeze.

The date palm is a 'cultigen', a plant known only in its cultivated form and domesticated for so long – at least 6,000 years – that no wild progenitor has ever been identified. Dried specimens have been recovered from archaeological sites dating back to the second millennium BCE. Strictly speaking it is not a real tree (there is no wood in the fibrous stem) but in many respects the date palm behaves like a tree. It is dioecious, with male and female flowers on separate palms. Pollination of the flowers is often artificially aided by introducing male flowers into female trees by hand. Clusters of the familiar fruit are huge, containing up to 1,500 dates on each stem; and a mature, productive tree (older than about five to eight years) can produce between 60 and 70 kilos of fruit every year for sixty or seventy years.[3] The fruits are harvested by hand, experienced pickers climbing each tree with the aid of a waist belt and using a special reaping hook. The potassium-rich fruits, when dried, keep extremely well and are exported round the world – a paragon of luxurious sweetness. They contain useful trace minerals, have a mild laxative effect and are said to be effective against respiratory diseases. Many cultivars have been developed locally for their sweetness and distinct flavour.

But the date palm is no one-trick pony. The seeds are soaked and then ground to make an animal feed. Sap is tapped from the stem and drunk fresh or fermented as the spirit 'arrack'. The leaves, symbolically important in Christian Easter festivities, make highly effective thatching, fencing and walling materials. Fibres from the leaves and 'bark' are useful in making ropes, baskets, hats and mats. Although not woody, the stem is termite-resistant and strong enough to be used in construction and for fuel. The date palm is also salt tolerant and often planted to reclaim land affected by salination.

FRUIT A PAIN

2

ARTOCARPUS incisus. Lin. f. S. XXI. 1. ex Ellis et nat. G.S.D.

The bounty of the Breadfruit
Artocarpus altilis

LOCAL NAMES: KURU (COOK ISLANDS); SUKUN (INDONESIA); UTO (FIJI)

Close to the harbour at Hope Town, on the eastern edge of the Bahamian Abaco islands, a plaque on a wall next to a splendid, venerable tree carries the following inscription:

> This breadfruit tree came from a supply of 2,126 plants transported from Tahiti to Jamaica in HMS *Providence* by Captain William Bligh, RN on his second Breadfruit voyage (1791–93). His first voyage ended in 1787 and resulted in the loss of 1,015 plants during the Mutiny on HMS *Bounty*. The plants carried by Captain Bligh to Jamaica were distributed throughout the Caribbean and the Americas as it was considered that the Breadfruit would provide a staple food for the settlers. It is a dietary staple much like potato that can be prepared by boiling, baking, roasting or frying.

The breadfruit is a native of New Guinea, probably transported by migrating seafarers across the remote islands of the Pacific Ocean. It bears very high yields of grapefruit-sized fruits rich in carbohydrates, vitamin C and potassium. The fruit being generally seedless, the tree is propagated from root cuttings. Joseph Banks, the naturalist who accompanied James Cook on his 1768–71 circumnavigation in HM Bark *Endeavour*, saw the potential of the tree to feed the slaves of the British Caribbean sugar trade. Returning to England, he encouraged and part-funded the notorious expedition undertaken in HMAT[4] *Bounty* under lieutenant William Bligh, Cook's former sailing master. Despite the disaster of the first voyage, Bligh succeeded in his second attempt to bring live specimens of the tree to the West Indies, where they flourished. Ironically, Banks's scheme ultimately fell foul of the slaves' dislike of the fruit.

Even so, the breadfruit qualifies as a supertree. Its timber is light and strong, resists shipworm and termites and was traditionally harvested for constructing houses and outrigger canoes. It also produces a latex, useful for trapping birds and caulking timber joints. Smoke from burning the dried flowers is an effective insect repellent. The leaves are fed to cattle as fodder and the wood can be pulped to make paper.

ARTOCARPUS.

J.Pass sculp.

The Bread Fruit Tree.

London, Published as the Act directs, Sept.3.1796. by J.Wilkes.

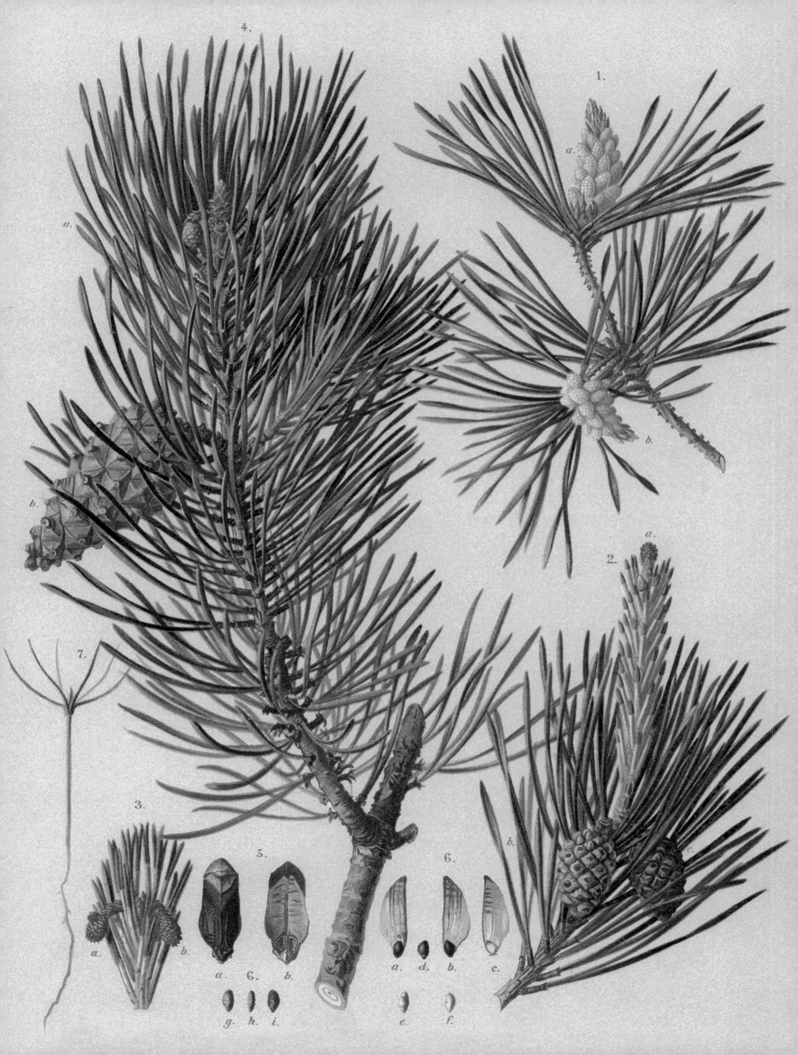

Scots pine
Pinus sylvestris

LOCAL NAMES: PIN SAUVAGE (FRENCH); WALDKIEFER (GERMAN); FURU (NORWEGIAN)

The magnificent Scots pine can be found across the Eurasian northern hemisphere, from Ireland to eastern Russia and as far south as northern Spain. In great swathes of forest or standing alone on a loch side, this eye-catching tree features deep-green 'clouds' of feathery, needle-laden branches and a reddish-brown scaly trunk. By nature gregarious, it supports below-ground mycorrhizal fungi, swapping sugars for scarce minerals and nitrogen in often impoverished soils. It was an early, genetically diverse colonizer of northern lands after the last Ice Age, thriving on and stabilizing glacial soils.

Wind-pollinated and monoecious, with separate male and female flowers on the same tree, it releases clouds of yellow pollen in spring, fertilizing the female cones of downwind trees, which ripen and open during autumn. The small seeds inside feed red squirrels and pine martens as well as a number of bird species.

Scots pines may grow to almost 45 metres (150 ft). Single specimens tend to grow with a spreading canopy, but they can take on diverse forms depending on altitude and exposure. They are cold tolerant and can thrive at up to 1,000 metres (3,300 ft) above sea level. Individual trees may live for up to 700 years, and the slowest-growing specimens in higher latitudes yield extremely fine, strong and workable timber with a pinkish tinge. As a fuel the wood burns well, having a high resin content. Mature natural woods, such as the remnants of the once extensive Caledonian forest, support a wide range of birds and insects, the deeply fissured trunks of older trees providing shelter. Specialized ground flora, such as the lesser twayblade orchid, thrive in these precious reserves.

Scots pines with straight, single trunks are cultivated for their timber from selected seed. They grow fast, up to half a metre (18 in) a year when young, and make effective windbreaks for farms and young plantations. The wood was once widely 'distilled' – burned in a very limited air supply – to make tar used in preserving timber and ships' cordage, with turpentine and charcoal as valuable by-products. As a large-scale biome, habitat, soil stabilizer and colonizer, and for its range of products, the Scots pine clearly qualifies as a supertree.

'Gold in them thar trees': the Eucalyptus
Eucalyptus spp.

LOCAL NAMES: GUM; COOLIBAH (KAMILAROI); MOUTAIN ASH

Picking just one eucalyptus species as a supertree out of the nearly 900 in existence is almost to miss the point. This genus of the fragrant myrtle family, so emblematic of Australia but now found across the globe, includes the tallest flowering plant on earth: the champion *Eucalyptus regnans*, called Centurion, stands at 100.5 metres (330 ft). Below ground, some eucalyptus roots penetrate so deep that they are able to concentrate deposits of mineral gold in their leaves.[5]

Eucalypts tend to be very fast-growing and drought-tolerant. The high levels of complex essential oils held in their leaves, bark and timber are both medicinally important and crucial in their role in promoting very fierce bush fires. The oils from various species (especially *E. globulus*) are used as antiseptics, solvents, insect-repellents and as a fragrance. The famed Blue Mountains of New South Wales are said to owe their colour to an atmospheric haze of isoprene produced by its eucalyptus forests.[6]

Long before Captain Cook's naturalist Sir Joseph Banks brought specimens back to Europe, Aboriginal Australians had developed a deep knowledge of the uses of these trees, said to cover some 92 million hectares (nearly 230 million acres) of Australia, each one adapted to a particular niche. Their flower nectar attracts bees that produce a dark amber honey; and all parts of the tree yield dyes. Small stems hollowed out by termites are used to make a traditional wind instrument, the didgeridoo. The seeds of the coolibah (*E. microtheca*) are edible; and indigenous hunter-gatherers collected and ate a sweet substance they called 'lerp', deposited on the leaves by insects to feed and protect their larvae.

The wood is valued for its rapid growth. Much is harvested for paper pulp, as a fuel, for charcoal production and to make fence posts. Since eucalypts are widely cultivated, there is considerable concern over the conservation of old stands of eucalyptus forest that provide important ecosystems for animals like the koala bear and possum, the larvae of many moths and other pollinating insects. Large-scale plantations in America, Africa and elsewhere are impacting adversely on the survival chances of their own indigenous species and biomes.

Mulga acacia
Acacia aneura

LOCAL NAMES: MULGA WATTLE; BOONAROO (AUSTRALIA)

Any species successfully colonizing the deserts of Australia must be tough, resilient and highly adapted. The thornless mulga acacia does not bear true leaves but flattened, thick-skinned pointed leaf stalks or phyllodes. They are covered in tiny hairs that grow very erect to minimize water loss in the intense midday sun. In very dry periods these phyllodes are shed, reducing water loss and acting as a protective mulch for the soil beneath the tree. Its minute stomata, through which it respires and exchanges gases with the atmosphere and which, on most trees, cover the undersides of the leaves, are hidden.

Sometimes growing as a shrub, sometimes as a tree that can reach heights of 15 metres (49 ft), the mulga acacia channels what little rain it receives down to the soil next to the base of its trunk, close to the deep, nitrogen-fixing roots that help to stabilize and enrich the soil. Acacia woodlands and scrub – important bush habitats across much of the continent – are often found close to seasonal stream-beds and on slopes and ridges. The seeds are dormant until germination is triggered by fire (a process called serotiny), but the parent tree does not survive the experience, nor does it recover from being cut down.

Unsurprisingly, perhaps, such a key plant has been exploited by equally tough and hardy Aboriginal Australians for tens of thousands of years. They used the dark, reddish-brown wood for shelter and firewood, to make digging sticks, spears and spear-throwers, clubs and boomerangs. European settlers opening up large areas of bush found it useful for fencing, furniture, carving and for turning objects on a lathe. The phyllodes were and are a valuable source of nutrition for grazing wildlife and stock throughout the year. The gall of a wasp that lays its larvae on the acacia was a bush-tucker food of Aboriginal hunter-gatherers and a gum exuded from branches was regarded as a sweet treat and a useful adhesive. Flour could also be ground from the seeds. The yellow flowers attract bees and their honey provides another vital nutritional resource for foraging groups. The mulga acacia, the Australian desert and its people seem perfectly suited to one another.

Fig. 3

A a transverse Section of the Jake fruit.
B The Seed.
C The Seed Surrounded with Pulp —

Jack of all trades: the Jackfruit
Artocarpus heterophyllus

LOCAL NAMES: JACA (PORTUGUESE, SPANISH); CHAKKA (MALAYLAM: INDIA); NANGKA (INDONESIAN)

OPPOSITE

A botanical illustration revealing the inside of a jackfruit by eighteenth-century artist James Kerr.

BELOW

Jackfruit growing out of the trunk of a tree in Motihar, western Bangladesh.

The jackfruit sits at the high table of the world's most useful trees. Domesticated several thousand years ago, it came to the notice of the Roman natural historian Pliny, and was described by admiring Jesuit missionaries in the seventeenth century. Cultivated in Southeast Asia, Africa, the Caribbean, South America and the Hawaiian Islands, the jackfruit is a tropical evergreen growing up to 25 metres (80 ft) tall. It bears the largest fruits of any tree – the record is a whopping 64 kilos (144 lbs) from a tree in Kerala, in its native India.[7] It produces latex, termite-resistant timber for furniture, barrels, musical instruments, Buddhist statues and house construction. In Hindu ceremonies a carved oval plank of jackfruit wood, called *avani palaka*, is used as a priest's seat. The heartwood yields a dye used in the manufacture of monastic robes, while the leaves are harvested as fodder for domestic livestock. The fruit is said to have a range of medicinal properties: as an astringent, an anti-inflammatory and antioxidant, although it seems that some of the more extravagant claims for its benefits lack scientific support.

Like the related breadfruit, it is as a culinary multi-tasker that jackfruit, in its many hybrid varieties, really shines. It grows directly from the trunk of the tree on a long, thick stem. Cut in half it looks like a pineapple and is said to smell like a combination of pineapple, banana and cheese, or even onions. The yellow arils inside the fruit, which can be individually prised out of the enveloping pulp, are fleshy, sickly sweet and very popular as desserts; when half-ripe they are an ingredient in curries. Slices of the fruit are sold from market stalls as snacks and are often deep-fried like potato chips. The gluten-free seeds can be pulped and used as flour or eaten dried. A single fruit may contain between 100 and 500 seeds.

Packed with carbohydrates, calcium and other useful minerals, the jackfruit is regarded by global agroforestry experts as a vital lifeline for subsistence farmers across the tropics and as a potentially valuable tree for intercropping and reforestation.[8]

D   C   B   A

Melaleuca ericifolia

June 1. 1805. Published by Ja.ˢ Sowerby, London.

Paperbark
Melaleuca spp.

LOCAL NAMES: NIAOULI (KANAK: NEW CALEDONIA); PUNK TREE (USA); WEEPING PAPERBARK (AUSTRALIA)

Ask the staff of the Department of Agriculture in the United States what they think of the paperbark tree and they will tell you that it is an invasive weed, rather too successfully naturalized in Florida as a means of helping to drain swamps and stabilize wet soils. But trees of the genus *Melaleuca*, some 300 species native to the east coast of Australia, Papua New Guinea and New Caledonia, are indispensable to their native cultures. Belonging to the myrtle family and remarkably tolerant of drought, cold and swampy ground, the paperbark bears leaves rich in essential oils. The timber is rot- and water-resistant and the easily peeled bark has many uses. The trees are planted for shade and for screening, while the timber is used for fence posts, telegraph poles and in parquet flooring.[9]

In early photographs, Aboriginal shelters often feature paperbark coverings. The thin sheets were used to line ovens, bedding areas and coolamans (multi-purpose wooden dishes with curved sides to carry everything from water to seeds and fruit and even for cradling babies) and, when wet, to wrap and cook perishable foods. The peeling bark is the tree's defence against fire. It quickly burns and falls away from the trunk, and shortly afterwards fresh green shoots appear as epicormic growth (sprouting directly from the trunk). The tree may live for 100 years or so, growing to between 9 and 15 metres (30–50 ft) tall.

Oils rich in antiseptic terpenes can be extracted by infusion from the leaves. Those of *M. quinquenervia* were traditionally used to treat headaches and colds, while the leaves of *M. alternifolia* produce tea-tree oil, famous around the world for its camphor-like smell and for treating skin conditions – even though it is toxic when swallowed and its effectiveness has not been scientifically proven. The oils also have uses in perfumery.

Nectar from the flowers of *M. quinquenervia* is washed out to make a sweet drink, while bees visiting the blooms produce a strongly flavoured amber honey. Fruit bats, lorikeets, flying foxes and many birds and insects are attracted to the flowers. On all fronts, the paperbark delivers.

The Cocoenut without y rinde

y Cocoa Nut tree

The Cocoenut with y Rinde

The younge Coco tree

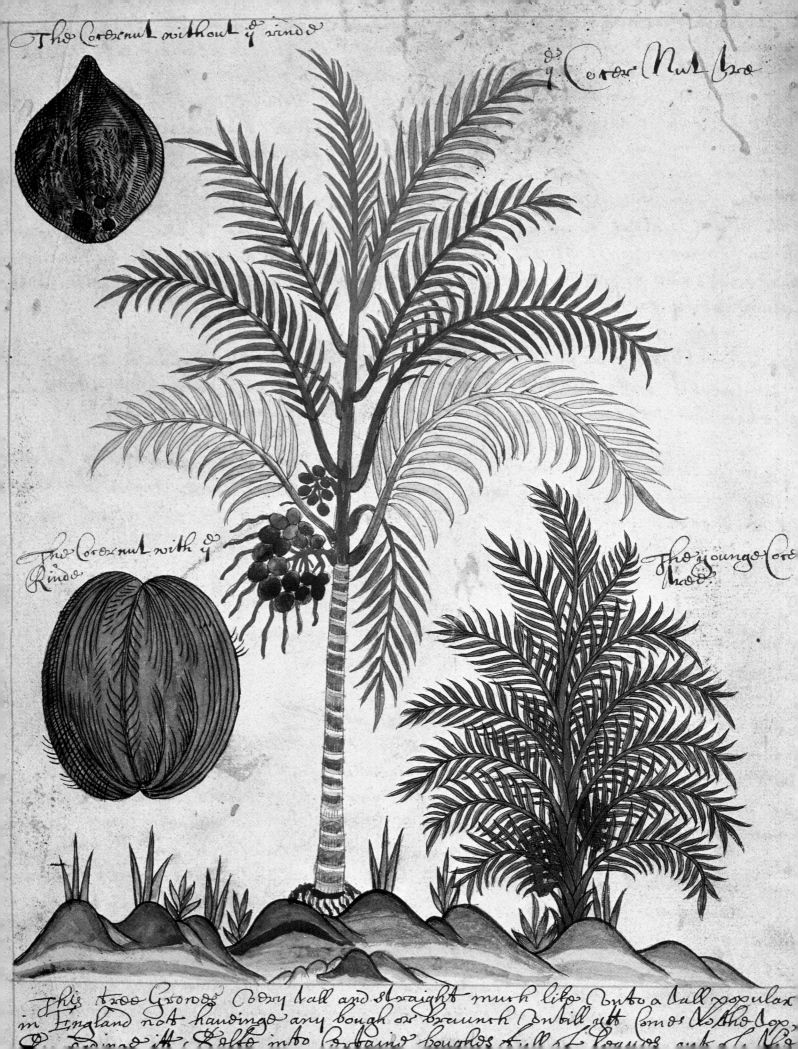

This tree groweth very tall and straight much like vnto a tall popular in England not hauinge any bough or braunch vntill vtt comes to the topp

Coconut palm
Cocos nucifera

LOCAL NAMES: NUX INDICA (LATIN); JAWZ HINDI (ARABIC)

OPPOSITE

An early botanical illustration of the coconut palm, from *A History of East Indian Trees and Plants, and of their Medicinal Properties*, 1600–1625.

BELOW

A solitary coconut palm, Bahia Honda, Florida Keys. *Cocos nucifera* is tolerant of salt spray.

OVERLEAF

Palm tree plantation in the Arabah (Arava), south of the Dead Sea basin.

Towards the end of his fifth voyage, the legendary Arab hero Sinbad the Sailor encountered a group of friendly merchants, with whom he went to collect coconuts. But the palm trees that bore them were so lofty, their trunks so smooth, that it seemed impossible to climb them. Instead, the merchants threw stones at the apes who sat chattering in their tops; the apes, joining battle, bombarded them with coconuts and Sinbad and his friends made a great profit, trading them for exotic aloe wood and pepper from the Spice Islands.[10]

The image of tall palms gracing a pristine beach, their feathery fronds waving in the breeze, is emblematic of equatorial oceanic islands from the Caribbean to Australia. The thin-rooted palms are perfectly adapted to salty air and thin, sandy soils and their skull-sized brown nuts are celebrated circumnavigators, carried to new lands by both ocean currents and, more reliably, early seafarers.

Coconuts are justly celebrated for the contents of the shell – both flesh and juice. The former is rich in fats, proteins and minerals – especially manganese, selenium and phosphorus. The latter is refreshing, low in calories and sweet. The flesh is eaten raw and used widely in cooking, adding sweetness to soups, stews and desserts, while the milk produced from the flesh makes a distinctive creamy thickener for curries. The oil is used for frying and in soap-making and has medicinal properties. And the coconut palm has yet more to offer: fresh growing buds, known as palm cabbage, are eaten as a delicacy while a sap produced by the flower clusters is drunk as *neera* or toddy, or fermented to produce wine. The leaves are used for thatching and weaving mats.[11]

Harvesting is, despite the testimony of Sinbad, mostly conducted by experienced climbers with a good head for heights (up to 30 metres/98 ft); but in Thailand and Malaysia trained pig-tailed macaques are sometimes employed. Coir, the natural fibrous wrapping for the husk, is used in matting and as a compost, while the shells make handy containers and cups. Charcoal produced by burning them is both a useful fuel and an effective filter of impurities in water. The 'timber' is used in the construction of houses, bridges and boats.

Tab. 472

Jatropha Curcas. L.

Supertree… or chimera?
The Physic nut
Jatropha curcas

LOCAL NAMES: BUBBLE BUSH; PURGING NUT

OPPOSITE

The twigs, leaves, flowers and fruit of the physic nut, as depicted in a six-volume study of medicinal plants by the German botanist Johannes Zorn, published in Amsterdam in 1796.

BELOW

The poisonous leaves of the physic nut.

BOTTOM

The fruit of the physic nut.

The physic nut presents humanity with a dilemma. For some it is a miraculous, oil-producing solution to the world's fossil-fuel crisis. For others its more locally practical virtues make it an all-purpose hardware store for fuel, lighting, varnish, soap, dyes and rat poison. Oil cake made from the pressed seeds is a valuable fertilizer and the leaves can be fed to the tusser silkworm.[12] But for some sceptics the idea of the physic nut as supertree is a chimera.

There is no doubting the ease of cultivation of this drought-tolerant Central American and Caribbean native, now grown widely across semi-arid regions of the world. It is propagated easily from seed to produce a manageable shrub up to 6 metres (20 ft) tall, yields oil from its seeds after a year or two and produces 1 to 12 tonnes of oil per hectare for over thirty years.[13] It can be used to recover contaminated or exhausted land and to 'green' deserts in countries like Egypt.

The seeds and leaves are poisonous to humans and livestock; but latex extracted from the bark contains jatrophine, credited with anti-carcinogenic properties. The oil is a proven biofuel and commercial airlines have successfully burned it as jet fuel. In Indonesia during the Second World War planting jatropha for production of oil as an industrial lubricant was compulsory. Herein lies the dilemma. Alternatives to crude oil are attractive, especially since the carbon released in the burning of biodiesel ought to be absorbed in equal measure by growing plants. And if jatropha is grown only on land unsuitable for other forms of cultivation, its large-scale planting and processing looks like a win–win situation – especially since it provides valuable cash income in precisely those parts of the world subject to the most environmental and social stress. On the other hand, critics say that in reality, widespread deforestation – itself a multi-effect ecological event – is the actual result of quick payback biomass cultivation schemes that replace genuine subsistence farming and local biodiversity. The jury may be out on biofuels but there is no doubting the remarkable nature of the physic nut tree.

Sal
Shorea robusta

LOCAL NAMES: SAL (GUJARATI); SALA (ASSAMESE; HINDI)

'Ananda, please prepare a bed for me between the twin sal-trees, with its head to the north. I am tired and will lie down.' These were the last words of the dying Buddha, some four hundred years before the birth of Christ. His mother is said to have given birth to him while holding a branch of the tree, while in Hindu tradition, the goddess Sarna Burhi inhabits a grove of sal trees.

The sal blooms with small, pale-grey velvety flowers with orange hearts, but only briefly – a proverbial symbol of the transitory nature of human existence and pride. This tall, spreading, gregarious evergreen is a feature of forest canopies, growing up to 35 metres (115 ft) tall. Its rich, lush foliage with large oval leaves provides continuous cover over many parts of northern India and southwest China. The clusters of ash-like seeds look like shuttlecocks before they fall, propeller-like, to the ground. The sal was always prized for its dense and durable tannin-rich timber, with dark reddish-brown heartwood and lighter sapwood. It is resistant to termite attack, easily sawn but hard to plane or nail because of its high resin content. It is a wood for engineers and house builders rather than sculptors, although locally it is coppiced to produce regular straight poles for a variety of domestic purposes, such as fencing and lightweight construction. The large, waxy leaves, well-suited to shedding monsoon rains, are widely used as plates and cups and for wrapping food; they are also browsed by passing ruminants.

Resin, known as 'lal dhuna', exuded from wounds in the bark and tapped commercially, has its own value as an incense, as a caulk for ship's planking, and in medicine for treating dysentery and gonorrhoea.[14] Oil from the seeds is used for lighting and cooking and in the treatment of skin conditions, while the seeds themselves are often boiled to make a porridge or ground into a coarse flour. Cakes made from the seeds, which are rich in starch, proteins and minerals, are sometimes used as a feed for livestock. Like many other sacred trees, the sal may owe its mythical reputation to its usefulness and ubiquity in its native lands: a gift of nature, if not of the gods.

Strange fruit: the argan
Argania spinosa

LOCAL NAMES: ARGAN (BERBER)

In the coastal forests of Atlantic Morocco the thorny branches of the spreading argan seem to bear strange fruit in late summer. Domestic goats perch precariously on slender branches, browsing on its leaves and appearing to watch the world go by while generally looking pleased with themselves. By this time of year most of the argan's highly valued nuts have fallen and been collected; women's co-operatives process them to produce a rich, fatty oil used in cooking as an alternative to the olive.

The long-lived argan has a highly adapted and deeply penetrating root system: it is drought tolerant and able to thrive in poor soils.[15] The soft fleshy fruits, looking like large acorns when unripe, are fed to goats and cattle alike as a food supplement. The nuts are cracked between stones to yield two or three seeds, which are roasted and ground with a little water in a stone quern. The resulting paste is squeezed to extract an oil, rich in vitamin E, with culinary, medicinal and cosmetic virtues first praised by the thirteenth-century Arab traveller and botanist Ibn Al-Baytar.[16] The leftover paste makes a seed cake rich in fat and protein. The roasted nuts keep well and form a vital food store to carry communities through lean times. The flowers are attractive to wild bees that nest in the trees and provide honey. Any fruit lying uncollected is eaten by goats, camels and cattle, inadvertently propagating a new generation of trees by excreting the seeds. Nut shells are burned as a fuel on domestic fires.

The argan is recognized as a keystone species in North Africa, providing shade with its dense canopy, soil protection and browsing. The insect-resistant timber is used in carpentry, as firewood and charcoal for fuel and plays a pivotal role in the regional cash economy: a sustainable ecological balance between humans and wildlife. That partnership is fragile – overgrazing by goats has to be controlled by wardens and rights to collect the fruits are carefully negotiated through family and community custom. Farmers clearing the forest for arable land are a threat. The 8,000 square kilometres or so of argan forest remaining in Morocco have been designated a UNESCO biosphere reserve. Commercial plantations have been established in Morocco, Jordan and Israel.

CHAPTER 6

Trees for the planet

A SELECT GROUP OF SPECIES, WHICH MIGHT ALSO include the argan, the alders and the sea buckthorn, belong to a special category of trees whose relationship to the land is as interesting and important as their specific value to humans. Many of them have been brought to global attention by the agroforestry movement, which places great emphasis on complementary suites of plants. Modern farming is increasingly monocultural, with the attendant potential for crop or market failure doing little to ensure that small, especially marginal, communities remain sustainable. In the West it is common to see livestock excluded from woodland, vegetable plot separated from orchard, grain from root crop. These distinctions are, in fact, relatively recent.

In permaculture or forest gardening traditions trees, bushes, vegetables and grain crops work in mutually beneficial 'guilds' that offer not only increased yields and a wider variety of dietary options but have also been shown to maintain healthy soils, stabilize riverbanks and sand dunes and protect wider biomes. Some are even able to detoxify soils poisoned by industrial waste or salination, and act as pioneers in reclaiming farmland from desert. Many local initiatives around the world have either inherited or re-invented agroforestry practices such as alley-cropping and interplanting, and the results during the last twenty or thirty years have been dramatic and impressive.

The loss of mangrove forests in Southeast Asia to shrimp farming and commercial harvesting for charcoal became the focus of world-wide attention in the aftermath of the December 2004 Indian Ocean tsunami. The effects of droughts and deforestation on marginal communities in the Sahel and sub-Saharan Africa has shown that over-dependence on a small selection of cash crops denudes soils, impoverishes village communities and contributes to habitat loss and climate change.

Several of the trees listed here are special because of their highly adapted root systems which, in the case of the legumes, fix atmospheric nitrogen and make it available to other plants. Some trees work well with root and vegetable

crops because their natural cycles are complementary and because the range of products that they supply balances seasonal and disease-related shortages, fostering co-operative community relations. If many of these trees are modest in looks or size, their value to the human–natural ecological partnership is enormous. Others are so highly adapted that they alone can thrive in extreme environments, providing large-scale biomes, climatic stability and natural wonders in their own right.

Around the world, schemes to replant trees and re-establish forest environments on country-wide or regional scales have often proved unsuccessful when organized by sometimes distant authorities intent on delivering a grand scheme. More success has been achieved with initiatives driven by small, local groups of food producers seeking repeatable, low-cost and labour-saving solutions that show small benefits quickly – and several of the trees in this section, especially the gao and mangrove, demonstrate these benefits.

Agroforestry is, above all, about practicalities. It starts with thinking about and looking after soil – preventing erosion, maintaining or enhancing nutrients and moisture retention, spreading risk across several species and experimenting creatively with suites of plants that work together in sometimes surprising ways. Often, such experiments have drawn on older traditions whose social and economic value has been forgotten in the rush for global economic growth. A huge store of local and traditional knowledge can be drawn on, often by the simple expedient of observing good practice and listening to traditional lore.

Sometimes, lessons learned in one environment have been successfully exported to other countries; on other occasions too little thought has been given to the environmental consequences – one farmer's miracle crop is another's weed. Nevertheless, in the history of our relations with trees, the lessons being learned by the global agroforestry movement are of immense importance for the future.

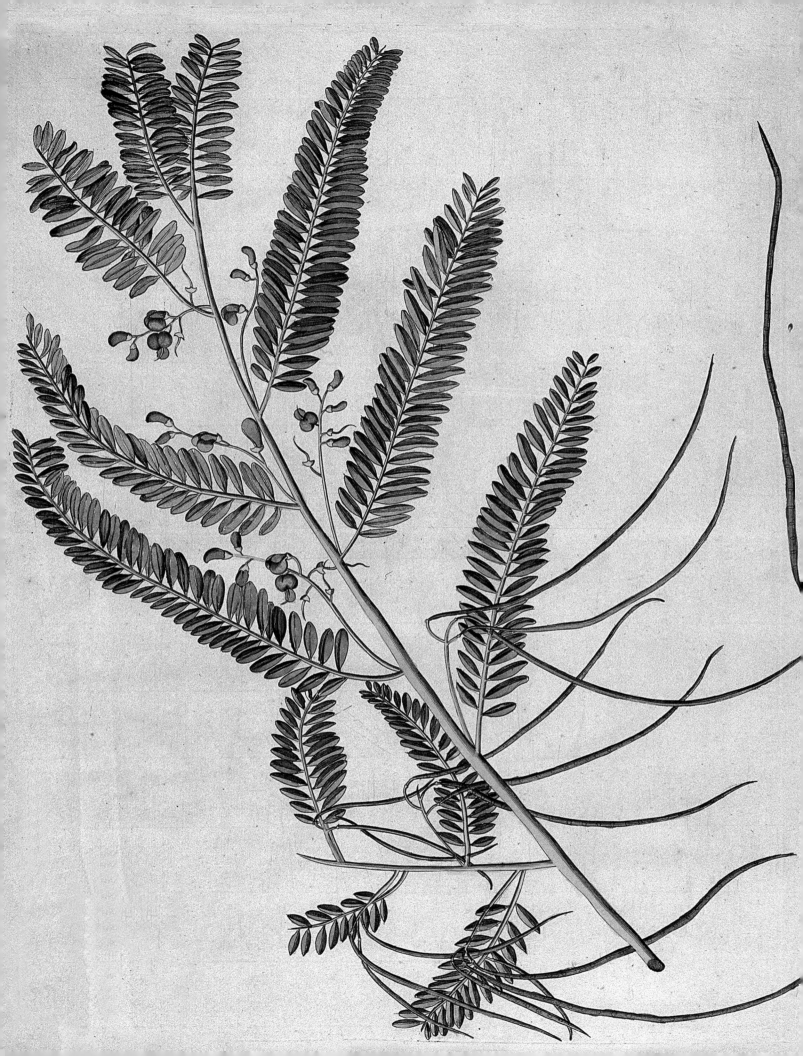

Sesbania
Sesbania sesban

LOCAL NAMES: RIVIERBOONTJIE (AFRIKAANS); SESABAN (ARABIC); UMQUAMBUQWEQWE (ZULU)

OPPOSITE

Sesbania twig, leaves, flowers and pods in a coloured engraving in *Hortus Malabaricus*, a comprehensive study of the flora of India's Western Ghats by Hendrik van Rheede, published 1678–93.

BELOW

The bi-pinnate leaves and pea-like flowers of the Sesbania are characteristic of leguminous, nitrogen-fixing trees.

Many of the ecological gems of the tree world are modest in size and looks. They are easily overlooked when compared to the soaring canopy trees of the temperate or tropical forests. The sesbania, native to East and North Central Africa but widely planted in southern Asia and Australia, is barely more than a shrub, growing to little more than 7 metres (22 ft) in height. Often found growing naturally on stream banks, the sesbania features compound leaves arranged like herringbones, yellow trumpet-like flowers and tell-tale hanging seed pods; all mark it out as a nitrogen-fixing legume – a relative of the pea.

The sesbania's value to the subsistence farmer is not confined to its soil-improving characteristics. It grows quickly, coping well with waterlogging and periodic flooding, helps to maintain riverbank stability and tolerates salty and alkaline soils. It is grown for shade, as a windbreak and as an intercropping plant, producing green manure and compost for agroforestry. It coppices readily to produce abundant, protein-rich fodder for cattle, sheep and goats in areas of otherwise poor grazing – although, oddly, its leaves are poisonous to hen chicks. The wood burns well as a fuel, kindling quickly and burning hot with little smoke; and it makes good charcoal. The flowers and seeds are edible.

Fibres from the sesbania are extracted and twisted for cordage and fishing nets, while bark and seeds both produce a useful gum. Fresh leaves and roots are employed in the treatment of scorpion stings and, by the Hausa of Nigeria, to help prevent tsetse fly infestations in cattle. Among indigenous pastoralists an infusion of the leaves is thought to have antibiotic and anti-carcinogenic properties.[1]

The fragile ecosystems inhabited by so many environmentally marginal communities around the world are vulnerable to the vagaries of climate, regional conflict and degradation by commercial and industrial interests. Integrating trees like sesbania with other subsistence strategies can mean the difference between famine and sustaining life. Traditional plant knowledge supported by science and investment may help to tip the balance in favour of communities who best understand how to exploit such special plants.

A miracle of a tree: the Moringa
Moringa oleifera

LOCAL NAMES: MLONGE (SWAHILI); MURUNGAI; DRUMSTICK; HORSERADISH

OPPOSITE
Moringa leaves and flowers in California's Riverside County.

BELOW
The pods, flowers and seeds of the moringa, in a seventeenth-century coloured line engraving.

OVERLEAF
Moringa plantation in Maharashtra, western peninsular India. Agroforesters have high hopes for its many virtues.

Many claims are made for the virtues of the unprepossessing but tough and resilient moringa – or 'miracle' tree. One writer has called it 'a supermarket on a trunk'.[2] Powder made from its seed pods is sold around the world as a superfood. Those same seeds may hold the key to decontaminating water supplies in the developing world.

The moringa, which is generally deciduous but which may in some conditions keep its leaves year round, is not much to look at, never growing more than about 12 metres (40 ft), with an open crown and drooping branches. Clusters of fragrant white flowers are followed by long thin seed pods reminiscent of drumsticks – hence one of its local names. In areas of high temperatures and low rainfall it comes into its own: it is fast growing, soil-improving and easily propagated from seeds or cuttings. Within a couple of years of planting it becomes productive, and a mature tree may produce 1,000 pods in a season. In India, perhaps its native land, a hectare of moringa will produce 30 tons of pods and 6 tons of vitamin- and mineral-rich leaves – not unlike spinach – in a single season's harvest. Oil from the pods is used as a food supplement and in the preparation of cosmetics and skin ointments. The flesh of the pods is a highly nutritious staple in curries, and the seeds are eaten dried and roasted, like nuts. The roots, with a flavour reminiscent of horseradish – suggesting another of the tree's nicknames – are used to make a condiment, while bark, sap, leaves and flowers are used in traditional medicine. The bark can be pulped to make paper. The seeds contain an antibiotic and fungicide, pterygospermin.

Much has been made of the moringa's potential in impoverished environments as a sustainable food crop, a living hedge, a nutrition-providing 'nurse' for other plants, as well as a tree that can help to counter desertification. But perhaps the moringa's most significant potential lies in the remarkable property of cakes made from its seeds to help decontaminate and purify water – a keystone of disease-prevention across the developing world. The moringa, a native of Southeast Asia, is now widely cultivated across Africa and South America.

Fishing with the Leichhardt
Nauclea orientalis

LOCAL NAMES: CHEESEWOOD; EXPLORER'S TREE; KANLUANG (THAILAND)

If you ever find yourself lost, alone and hungry in Australia's Northern Territories or in the Indonesian archipelago, a knowledge of the local plants – knowledge drawn on by indigenous people for thousands of years – will stand you in good stead. The eye-catching globular, flower clusters of the Leichhardt tree set against dark waxy leaves may be your best clue to a nice fish supper, since its bark contains toxins that have a stupefying effect on fish. Scrape a piece of the creamy brown bark off and throw it into the nearest pond or stream, then watch the stunned fish float to the surface. Light a fire and cook to taste.

The Leichhardt is an impressive tree all round. It stands tall, up to 30 metres (98 ft), often with a single straight trunk before it branches out into a spreading, sometimes conical canopy. Perfectly suited to lowland tropical forest environments, this tree is tolerant of both shade and flood. The Leichhardt is regarded as a pioneer species for land reclamation.

The leaves, deciduous in a prolonged dry season, have prominent yellow veins. The flowers attract nectar-loving insects and birds such as honeyeaters. The spherical, brown compound fruits are bitter but edible – and much loved by yellow orioles and flying foxes – while a drink made from crushed fruit is a traditional treatment for diarrhoea and fever. Leichhardt wood is an attractive soft yellow in colour. It carves easily, will resist termite attack and is used for lightweight construction, although it is not regarded as durable outside.

The tree was named in honour of the enigmatic German explorer and naturalist Ludwig Leichhardt (1813–c.48). He made three great expeditions into the interior of Australia; on the second, from 1844 to 1846, he triumphantly turned up in Port Essington (near modern Darwin) after a journey of some 3,000 miles across the outback from Queensland, having been given up for dead. After a third expedition in 1846, frustrated by hunger and fever, he set out again in 1848 with the aim of reaching the Swan River in Western Australia, crossing the great desert of the interior. The last sight of the expedition was on the Darling downs some 80 miles to the west of Brisbane. The remains of the party have never been found.

White lead tree
Leucaena leucocephala

LOCAL NAMES: HUĀXCUAHUITL (NAHUATL); JUMBIE BEAN, SUBABUL (HINDI); LUSINA (KISWAHILI)

OPPOSITE
White lead tree twigs, leaves and pods in a botanical illustration by Spanish botanist and friar Francisco Manuel Blanco (1778–1845).

BELOW
White lead tree flowers resemble miniature fireworks displays.

The sesbania of East Africa has a Central South American counterpart, another multi-tasking herring-bone-leaved legume; but it is not without its detractors. The white lead tree is fast-growing – reaching 10 to 15 metres (33 to 49 ft) in just a few years – coppices readily and fixes nitrogen in the soils where it grows. The leaves are used as fodder for cattle, the wood for fuel, paper pulp and poles, the roots for medicine and the bark for tannin and dyestuffs. The tree acts as an effective windbreak and in Uganda it is widely planted as a host for vanilla orchids.[3] The seed pods are eaten, especially in Southeast Asia and in Mexico.

In landscapes where there is a prolonged dry season the browsing value of tree foliage for hard-pressed cattle can hardly be exaggerated – it may mean the difference between life and death and the sustainability of communities who rely on those cattle for their livelihoods. Experiments conducted in Africa's Rift Valley comparing *Leucaena* with other useful browsing trees show that it offers significantly higher yields of milk and meat than many other species, when used as a fodder crop for grazing herds than many other species.[4] It grows readily from seeds, which are naturally dispersed and fertilized by animals and birds and along waterways.

But that readiness to propagate has resulted in *Leucaena*'s darker reputation as an uncontrollable invader. Despite its evident virtues, it sits on a list of the world's 100 worst weeds. In South Africa biological pest control is used to limit its spread. The amino acid mimosine produced in the leaves is poisonous or indigestible to some non-ruminants. The tree is also susceptible to attack by psyllid lice.

Trees with such ambivalent value to the planet are sometimes termed 'conflict' trees. Their spread and exploitation raise all sorts of questions about human manipulation of the environment and about bio-security. For every human benefit gained by introducing novel species, it seems that nature finds a way of wagging its finger at those who interfere with its finely balanced regime.

The Chachafruto
Erythrina edulis

LOCAL NAMES: BASUL (ANDEAN REGION); PISONAY (PERU, ARGENTINA); GUATO (ECUADOR)

In the pre-Columbian societies of the Andes, indigenous knowledge and exploitation of plants reached an extraordinary level of sophistication. Potatoes, tomatoes and chocolate are now global staples; but, many of their most useful plants were under-utilized and ignored by conquering Europeans and have attracted relatively little scientific attention. Only in recent decades has this uniquely diverse source of knowledge and cultivation practice been recognized more widely by researchers.[5]

With renewed interest in sustainable agroforestry, attention has turned to a leguminous tree of the Andes, the chachafruto or basul. Deciduous, it grows to about 10 metres (33 ft) and is ideally suited to high-altitude tropical lands. Easily spotted in the flowering season by its spiky scarlet blooms and then by the huge bean pods that hang from its branches, the chachafruto is a soil-improving, food-producing miracle.

The tree is easily propagated from cuttings, seeds and grafting, a great advantage for small, independent growers. After three or four years it begins to flower and yield abundant, large green edible pods. More usually, the pods are allowed to ripen before harvesting. The trees may be productive for decades, given enough sunlight. Pods remain on the tree even while a new season's flowering has begun, so they can be picked almost year round. The beans are pleasantly sweet and protein-rich, with a high potassium content. They must be boiled to remove toxic alkaloids, but can then be dried and milled to make a flour to be stored for later use. Nutritional scientists are increasingly excited about the beans' anti-oxidant properties and their propensity to remove dietary toxins. Animals can be fed on pods, cooked beans and leaves.

The chachafruto has never been cultivated commercially, but is highly valued by small communities of farmers for whom it is a key component in their subsistence strategies. This productive tree is also interplanted with coffee for its shade and nitrogen-fixing roots, used as a highly effective thorny fence and, when felled, for firewood and small timber.

OPPOSITE

Chachafruto tree in blossom, Cuenca, Ecuador.

BELOW

Detail of chachafruto flowers, growing near the city of Armenia, Colombia.

Kauri
Agathis australis

LOCAL NAMES: KAURI (MAORI)

On 24 December 1835, an English naturalist wrote in his journal:

A little before noon Messrs. Williams and Davies walked with me to part of a neighbouring forest, to show me the famous kauri pine. I measured one of these noble trees, and found it thirty-one feet in circumference above the roots… These trees are remarkable for their smooth cylindrical boles, which run up to a height of sixty, and even ninety feet, with a nearly equal diameter, and without a single branch. The crown of branches at the summit is out of all proportion small to the trunk; and the leaves are likewise small compared with the branches. The forest was here almost composed of the kauri; and the largest trees, from the parallelism of their sides, stood up like gigantic columns of wood. The timber of the kauri is the most valuable production of the island; moreover, a quantity of resin oozes from the bark, which is sold at a penny a pound to the Americans, but its use was then unknown.[6]

Charles Darwin, on his second voyage in HM Sloop *Beagle*, was not the last to be impressed by this giant of the ancient Antipodean forest, a native of the northern part of North Island, New Zealand, and a relative of the Chilean pine or Monkey Puzzle tree *Araucaria araucana*. Kauris form forests with a canopy 50 metres (164 ft) above ground level and, as Darwin observed, the trunks are conspicuously massive.

The kauri is a keystone species: over many millions of years it has helped to create a unique ecological niche. It sheds its lower branches, and scales from its bark accumulate in great heaps around the base of the trunk, so that it remains free from parasitic climbers. Its litter is acidic and podzolizes the soil to deter all but very specialized plants from competing with it for nutrients. Like the beech and Scots pine, the kauri forms a relationship with mycorrhizal fungi in the soil, swapping scarce trace minerals with sugars generated by its leaves in photosynthesis. Those plants that can live with the kauri help to create a unique biome.

Despite widespread logging of the kauri for its high-quality timber – used in construction and shipbuilding – by European settlers, it survives in protected areas such as the Waipoua forest. Two giant specimens, Tane Mahuta and Te Matua Ngahere, are venerated by Maoris and have become popular tourist attractions.

Friends in need: Mangroves
Rhizophora

LOCAL NAMES: MANGUE (PORTUGUESE); TONGO (TONGAN)

The lives of at least 10,000 people were saved during the Boxing Day tsunami of 2004 because their coastal settlements were protected by the mangal, a diverse marine plant biome dominated by the weird-looking but brilliantly adapted mangrove. In the Indonesian province of Aceh, which bore the devastating brunt of the tsunami, millions of trees have since been planted in the shallow coastal mud where salt-tolerant mangroves thrive.[7] When established they will provide a protective belt, absorbing much of the energy of tidal surges and storm waves, protecting vulnerable coastal habitats and communities from their worst effects and slowing or halting erosion. Mangal destruction is a pivotal driver of global deforestation and the degradation of biodiverse habitats; replanting does not remedy the immense loss of its diverse ecologies.

The mangal biome is found across the world, from Central America to China, from the Gulf of Oman to the southern tip of Australia. When thriving and carefully managed, mangal offers sustainable harvests of fuel, timber and medicines; supporting many species of marine creatures and abundant bird and insect life. This precious habitat has, however, been denuded over the last few decades by clearing for shrimp farms and the felling of trees for commercial production of charcoal, leaving coastlines unprotected and their dependent communities reliant on aid or cash crops.

The diverse mangal species that thrive in warm, salty, shallow waters are made up of shrubs and small trees, of which fifty or so mangrove species are the best known. The red mangrove (*Rhizophora mangle*), perhaps the most distinctive of these, is propped up above standing tidal waters by its bizarre-looking leggy roots. Oxygen is taken in through these aerial roots and through pores in the bark, to help drive a complex desalination process in its cells. Any excess salt is concentrated in older leaves, to be shed by the tree. The spear-shaped seed pods of the mangrove are buoyant and can germinate while still attached to the tree; if they fall on soft mud they make ready-prepared seedlings.

We need mangroves and their habitats: they represent a vital organic resource for the planet.

The survivor: Dahurian larch
Larix gmelinii

LOCAL NAMES: GUI-NATSU (JAPANESE)

In winter, on the Taymyr peninsula in the far north of Russia, the average temperature is -33 °C. Two large mammals, the musk ox and reindeer, thrive in these latitudes and provide a means of subsistence for the nomadic Nenets people. Here also, where the great boreal forest or taiga, the world's greatest land biome, meets the arctic tundra, the Dahurian larch is the last tree standing. It is the most northerly and the most cold-hardy tree on the planet.

Larches (more than a dozen species) are deciduous conifers – not quite a contradiction in terms. They grow pine-like needles in a spectacular green flush in spring. In autumn the needles turn yellow and are then shed, allowing the larch to withstand heavy snowfalls. It loses much of its water content too, to protect against hard frosts. The Dahurian larch can grow to about 30 metres (98 ft) in height, with the typical conical structure of a tree adapted to the low sun of extreme latitudes – up to 70° N, well inside the Arctic Circle, where there is no direct sunlight for several weeks in winter. The Dahurian larch, as a result, is very slow-growing: the most ancient specimen so far measured was 916 years old, its seed germinating some time in the eleventh century.

Further south, the Dahurian larch forms an almost continuous forest belt around the planet, in partnership with pines, spruces and hardier deciduous trees like birch, alder and willow. Compared to the tropical rainforests, the boreal forest habitat may seem impoverished; but thanks to its once marginal value to farming peoples its special plant, animal and human cultures have remained relatively intact into modern times. The magnificent landscapes of the untouched taiga of Asia and North America are one of the world's great natural wonders. The taiga's sheer size allows vast areas of specialized habitat to thrive on a scale matched nowhere else on earth. Increasingly, though, even here, the land is under pressure for the exploitation of oil, gas and timber.

The larch's botanical name celebrates the pioneering work in Northern Russia of botanist Johann Georg Gmelin (1709–55). Scientists have recently begun to extract from it a natural antioxidant (taxifolin) known to inhibit the growth of cancer cells.

TAMARINIER,

Tamarindus Indica, L.

The 'Indian date': Tamarind
Tamarindus indica

LOCAL NAMES: TAMARINDO (LATIN AMERICA); SAMPALAK (FILIPINO)

OPPOSITE

Tamarind tree in a hand-coloured engraving after a botanical illustration by Édouard Maubert for *Le Règne végétal*, published in Paris, 1864–71.

BELOW

The dense, many-branched canopy of a tamarind tree.

The tamarind has everything: looks, longevity, abundant exotic-looking fruit and many practical virtues. It might well be a supertree, but makes it into this chapter because, as a legume, it has the special virtue of fixing atmospheric nitrogen in impoverished soils. It is tolerant of wind, salt, drought and heat – indeed, of most conditions that nature can throw at a tree, apart from frost.[8] A native of the tropics of Africa, it has been established for so long elsewhere that medieval Arab traders extolling the virtues of its sweet, sticky fruit thought of it as the 'Indian date', or *tamr hindi*.

The tamarind grows tall (up to 30 metres/98 ft), with a spreading crown of herringbone-pattern leaves and branches all along its trunk. By the age of seven to ten years it produces beautiful, delicate red-and-cream flowers which, when fertilized, bear the distinctive pea-like pods that betray its leguminous genes. An evergreen, the tamarind can nevertheless be coppiced, extending its productive life to 200 years or more. It is propagated from seed or by grafting. Two main varieties, one with acidic tasting pulp, the other rather sweeter, are widely cultivated.

The seed pods may be harvested while still green for a piquant seasoning; when fully ripe pods of the sweeter varieties contain the soft, sugary date-like pulp so popular in curries, pickles and chutneys. Two well-known condiments found on tables in Britain and across the world – Worcestershire sauce and HP sauce – rely on tamarind for their characteristic flavouring. The mineral and B-vitamin rich pulp has a mild laxative effect.

The bark is used in medicine as an astringent, to soothe sores and ulcers and to reduce fever. The leaves, which yield a red dye, have antioxidant properties and may reduce blood-sugar levels. They can also be drunk as an infusion.

Oil from the crushed seeds, which acts like linseed oil, is used in paint-making and in lamps for illumination. The sapwood of the tamarind is light yellow with a darker, harder and more durable heartwood, sometimes called Madeira mahogany. It is ideal for carpentry, wheel-making, tool-handle manufacture and furniture and for good-quality charcoal.

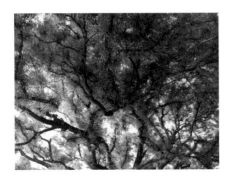

Gao
Faidherbia albida

LOCAL NAMES: BALANZAN (MALI: BAMBARA); APPLE-RING ACACIA; WHITE ACACIA; SAAS (SENEGAL: SERER)

A quiet miracle is transforming one of the most impoverished landscapes in Africa. Mamadou Diakité tells anyone who will listen how it started. In the 1980s, men from the Maradi region of Niger, which had suffered decades of drought, returned home after seasonal work abroad and planted seeds for their crops without clearing the scrub on their land. To everyone's astonishment their sorghum, millet, maize and vegetable crops grew better than those on the carefully cleared plots of their neighbours, where seeds often blew away in dust storms. Not clearing the trees seemed to be helping.[9] A generation later, millions of hectares in Niger have become green and productive again.

The gao is one of the key tree partners in this process. It has the odd distinction of shedding its leaves in the rainy season and growing them in the dry season, providing mulch and fertilizer, then shade, then full sun, precisely when grain and other food crops need them. For livestock, fodder is available when all other food has been used up. It's an adaptation called 'reverse leaf phenology' and it leads to double or triple yields for farmers.

Like many other agroforestry trees, the thorny gao is a legume, fixing atmospheric nitrogen in the soil around its roots and making it available to other plants nearby. It has the mimosa-like leaves and nutritious pods typical of the family *Fabaceae*. It can grow up to 30 metres (98 ft) tall, although it is often smaller and scrubbier in appearance.

As well as fostering good crop growth and holding back the desert, the gao supports foraging by domesticated and wild animals while the flowers, blooming when all else locally has died, are invaluable for bees and honey production. The wood is valued in the construction of canoes, utensils, drums, boxes and oil presses, though it tends to be too twisty for construction.[10] It makes good fuel and fine charcoal, and the wood ash is used in soap-making. The bark is used as an astringent. The seeds are, however, toxic to humans unless carefully processed. The tree can be propagated from seed or by cuttings. Along with other key tree species, the gao is supporting a local community revolution – just where it is needed.

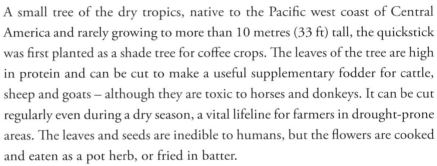

Quickstick
Gliricidia sepium

LOCAL NAMES: MADERON NEGRO (COSTA RICA); KAKAWATE (FILIPINO); WETAHIRIYA (SINHALESE)

A small tree of the dry tropics, native to the Pacific west coast of Central America and rarely growing to more than 10 metres (33 ft) tall, the quickstick was first planted as a shade tree for coffee crops. The leaves of the tree are high in protein and can be cut to make a useful supplementary fodder for cattle, sheep and goats – although they are toxic to horses and donkeys. It can be cut regularly even during a dry season, a vital lifeline for farmers in drought-prone areas. The leaves and seeds are inedible to humans, but the flowers are cooked and eaten as a pot herb, or fried in batter.

The herringbone-pattern leaves and tightly strung pink-and-white pea-like blossom of the quickstick are a horticultural giveaway. Like many of the most important subsistence trees, it is easily identified as a nitrogen-fixing legume able to release its fertilizing minerals to neighbouring plants. But the boost that its roots give to other food plants is only one of its many virtues.

Planted as an intercrop species with vegetables and in cashew orchards, the quickstick – as its nickname suggests – can be frequently coppiced for fuel, after which it enters a dormant phase allowing other plants to flourish without competition. Growing quickly, and easily propagated from the abundant seeds in its pods, the quickstick is a useful soil stabilizer, especially on steep slopes, and as a green manure plant to be sown after slash-and-burn clearance. The leaves are also used in the preparation of hair conditioners. The cut poles and living trees make good supports for climbing crops like black pepper, vanilla and yam. In Central America, farmers wash their livestock with a paste of crushed leaves to ward off the torsalo flies that torment them.

The quickstick is now widely planted in a global belt that spans Central Africa and Southeast Asia, where it is established to shade cocoa trees. In India, poles from the tree are used to create living fencing, protecting valuable fruit and vegetables from livestock and predators. The wood is hard and durable, burns with little smoke and makes good charcoal. It can be used in making railway sleepers, farm implements, tool handles and furniture.

A tree for a continent: Marula
Sclerocarya birrea

LOCAL NAMES: MGONGO (SWAHILI)

The marula is such a useful tree that it might comfortably sit in several sections of this book. It qualifies as a 'tree for the planet' because it is easily cultivated in the impoverished soils of those parts of Africa most subject to environmental fragility and consequent hardship: the Sahel countries of Mauritania and Senegal, across to Eritrea, Ethiopia, southeast to Uganda and Kenya and, in the southwest, Namibia and Botswana. A soil-improving tree that provides shelter from sun and wind, the marula is fast growing and sets fruit just three years after planting.[11]

The pale-green plum-sized fruits are eaten raw or cooked, as a thirst-quenching snack; elephants have been known to get drunk after gorging on them as they lie fermenting on the ground. Pulped, they produce jam, beer, wine or syrup and the only reason that they are not exported is a tendency to ripen quickly and bruise easily – making them difficult to store and transport. Paradoxically, this is advantageous to small communities that rely heavily on the marula for their subsistence. Although there are now commercial plantations in Israel, as a cash crop the tree is generally underexploited so that it forms a modest but significant and diverse role in localized agriculture strategies. The protein-rich seeds are said to taste like walnuts or peanuts; they also yield an oil used in cooking and in lamps.

The benefits of the marula extend to its bark: infusions are used in pain relief and to reduce inflammation and for stomach aches. Bark chips are chewed to relieve toothache. A paste made from the bark of the roots is rubbed onto snake-bite wounds. The roots themselves are pounded with water to make a drink said to treat symptoms of the parasitic infection schistosomiasis or bilharzia. As if this bounty were not sufficient, the bark can also be processed to make a fibre for ropes and a pinkish dye; and when cut it exudes a gum used to make ink. The wood is easily converted into bowls and carvings, drums and canoes. The marula, if not a tree for the whole planet, is nevertheless a tree for a continent – a vital community partner for millions of people across Africa.

abscission – the set of chemical processes by which deciduous trees extract nutrients from their leaves, seal them off from their twigs and then shed them in autumn.

agroforestry – a term used to describe the ntegration of trees with root, grain and fruit crops. In this system trees protect soil, provide shade, yield fodder and other supplementary crops with many often supplying valuable nitrogen to impoverished soils.

allelopathy – the propensity for some plants to inhibit growth in, or deter the presence of, other plants by the release of toxic chemicals. Some walnuts, eucalypts and the kauri are allelopathic.

alley-cropping – an agroforestry technique that involves planting lines of trees alternately with compatible ground-cropped vegetables or fruit. Benefits include pest control, soil moisture retention, shade, wind protection and supplementary subsistence products. Coffee is often grown as a companion plant in such systems.

angiosperms – the flowering plants that produce seeds within a carpel (female reproductive organ), including the deciduous trees.

apical bud – the leading skyward bud of a tree, from which the following year's vertical growth comes. The growth hormone auxin, concentrated here in many trees, suppresses latent lateral (side) buds from growing. When an apical bud is damaged or removed, as in pruning, coppicing or storm damage, the auxin is suppressed and new shoots spring from either the base or trunk of many trees.

coppice – the very ancient practice of cutting deciduous trees at the base on a regular cycle to produce manageable crops of poles and foliage for use in fencing, ovens and light construction. The word is Old French *copeiz*, from the medieval Latin *colpus*, meaning a blow.

cultigen – the term is used to describe trees whose separation by human cultivation from their wild forebears is so ancient that the evolutionary history cannot now be traced. Date palms and avocados are good examples.

dichogamy – in botany, the propensity of the male and female reproductive parts of a flower to ripen at different times, preventing self-fertilization. It is a very obvious phenomenon in some common monoecious trees, such as walnuts, alders and hazels, which have separate male and female flowers on the same tree. The pollen from one tree tends, then, to fertilize the female of another tree whose female flowers are already ripe.

dioecious – bearing male and female flowers on separate trees. The holly is a notable example.

epiphyte – generally, a plant that grows up another, like the strangling fig. It is not necessarily parasitic and often gains its water and nutrients from the atmosphere.

gregarious – the tendency for some trees to thrive in the company of their own species, like beeches and Scots pines, which share relations with mycorrhizal fungi below ground.

gymnosperm – literally, 'naked seed', this denotes a plant whose seed is unprotected by an ovary or fruit. It is applied to the conifers, the ginkgo and cycads and indicates a fundamentally different branch of the plants from the angiosperms.

hermaphrodite – in plants, a tree that bears flowers with both male and female parts. The custard apple is an example.

heterozygous – a word describing trees whose genes are mapped at random onto the chromosomes of their offspring, producing in effect a new variety in each generation. Apples and other trees that require grafting to maintain their characteristics are examples of heterozygy.

leguminous – a word describing plants belonging to the family *Fabaceae* or *Leguminosae*. Peas, beans and many trees are leguminous, bearing characteristic pods that contain their seeds, and often growing root nodules that fix atmospheric nitrogen, which is then made available to other plants.

lenticel – a pore appearing on the surface of the bark of many trees, through which the tree can exchange gases with the atmosphere in addition to the stomata (the minute holes on the underside of a leaf through which it exchanges water and gases with the atmosphere). Birch and cherry trees have very obvious lenticels, seen as lines of what look like horizontal scars on their trunks.

mast – the nuts of trees, especially the beeches and oaks, when they fall in large numbers in autumn. Livestock was traditionally turned out into beech and oak woods in autumn to fatten on mast – a practice called called pannage. Mast years are those in which such trees produce a superabundance of nuts.

monoecious – bearing separate male and female flowers on the same tree, like the catkins and cones of alders.

montado and dehesa – traditional agroforestry practices of southern Portugal and central southern Spain, in which livestock are grazed among trees. A form of wood pasturing, it fosters an open ecosystem that produces not just firewood, cork and other timber products, but also mushrooms, honey and the wild game that thrives in these woods.

mycorrhizal – a group of very fine tendril-like fungi that form symbiotic relations with certain trees, enhancing their potential to draw nutrients from poor soils in return for sugars that they harvest from the trees' roots. Beeches and Scots pines benefit from such fungi, a feature of gregarious trees.

parthenocarpic – a word describing 'virgin fruit' produced by a natural or artificially induced genetic ability to develop fruit without fertilization. Seedless fruits are parthenocarpic cultivars, as are those edible figs that do not require the services of a wasp to fertilize their flowers.

phloem – the plant tissues that conduct sugars, minerals and water to and from leaves and roots.

podzolize – to leach a soil of its mineral nutrients, through high rainfall.

pollard – a tree that has been coppiced above the height at which browsing animals can feed on new shoots, allowing a form of agroforestry known as wood pasture. Willows and alders are commonly seen as pollarded trees by rivers. From 'poll', an old word meaning 'to cut off the head of a tree or plant'.

pyrophyte – a plant adapted to tolerate fire, such as the cork oak and the desert quandong.

ENDNOTES

Chapter 1

1. Tully, J. 'A Victorian Ecological Disaster: Imperialism, the Telegraph, and Gutta-Percha', *Journal of World History* 20 (4), 2009, pp. 559–579
2. Gidmark, David *The Algonquin Birch Bark Canoe*, Shire Ethnography, 1988
3. http://tropical.theferns.info/viewtropical.php?id=Ceiba+pentandra
4. http://www.bradshawfoundation.com/thor/kon-tiki.php
5. http://sciencewise.anu.edu.au/articles/timbers
6. https://www.hydroworld.com/articles/hr/print/volume-33/issue-6/articles/back-to-our-roots-the-return-of-an-old-friend-for-turbine-bearing-rehab.html
7. http://tropical.theferns.info/viewtropical.php?id=Crescentia+cujete
8. https://archive.is/20060316012526/http://www.killerplants.com/plant-of-the-week/20050131.asp
9. http://www.euforgen.org/fileadmin//bioversity/publications/pdfs/1323_Cork_oak__Quercus_suber_.pdf
10. https://pfaf.org/user/Plant.aspx?LatinName=Quercus+suber
11. https://www.rainforest-alliance.org/species/rubber-tree
12. Nat Hist Museum on Slavery, pp.14-15
13. Lamb, FB *Mahogany of Tropical America: Its Ecology and Management*, University of Michigan Press, 1966, p. 10
14. *World Encyclopedia of Trees*, p. 174
15. See the entry on the Breadfruit tree.
16. http://powo.science.kew.org/taxon/urn:lsid:ipni.org:names:850861-1
17. http://tropical.theferns.info/viewtropical.php?id=Aleurites+moluccanus
18. http://canoeplants.com/kukui.html
19. http://tropical.theferns.info/viewtropical.php?id=Roystonea+regia
20. https://www.science.gov/topicpages/r/roystonea+regia+fruits.html

Chapter 2

1. Kauz, R. *Aspects of the Maritime Silk Road: From the Persian Gulf to the East China Sea*, 2010
2. https://worldneurologyonline.com/article/controversial-story-aspirin/
3. 'Logwood Dye on Paper', by Erin Hammeke, undated thesis for the University of Texas. https://www.ischool.utexas.edu/~cochinea/pdfs/e-hammeke-04-logwood.pdf
4. Dragon's blood: Botany, chemistry and therapeutic uses. *Journal of Ethnopharmacology* 115 (2008) 361–380.
5. *Taxus brevifolia*: https://www.conifers.org/ta/Taxus_brevifolia.php
6. Jon Henley, 'The mozzies are coming'. *The Guardian*, 12.8.2007 https://www.theguardian.com/society/2007/sep/12/health.weather
7. https://phys.org/news/2018-10-peru-danger-national-cinchona-tree.html
8. 'Phytopharmacology of Ficus religiosa'. https://www.ncbi.nlm.nih.gov/pmc/articles/PMC3249921/
9. https://www.japantimes.co.jp/life/2002/08/01/environment/a-camphor-by-any-other-name/#.XAZUGtv7TmE
10. https://en.wikipedia.org/wiki/Camphor
11. https://www.uaex.edu/yard-garden/resource-library/plant-week/sassafras.aspx
12. *Trees in Indian art, mythology and folklore*, 18; 20; 57ff. Bansi La Malla 2000, Aryan Books International
13. *Edible Trees*, pp. 13–14

Chapter 3

1. Howes, F. N. *Nuts: Their Production and Everyday Uses*, Faber and Faber, 1948, pp. 147–164
2. Howes 1948, p. 42
3. https://www.nytimes.com/2007/08/08/dining/08mang.html
4. Howes 1948, p. 100
5. 'Remains of seven types of edible nuts and nutcrackers found at a 780,000-year-old archaeological site.' http://www3.scienceblog.com/community/older/2002/F/20022752.html
6. http://tropical.theferns.info/viewtropical.php?id=Inocarpus+fagifer
7. http://www.agroforestry.net/images/pdfs/Inocarpus-Tahitianchestnut.pdf
8. *Luke* 13:6–9
9. https://en.wikipedia.org/wiki/Hortus_Malabaricus
10. https://www.telegraph.co.uk/news/earth/earthnews/5857472/Royal-Botanic-Gardens-mango-tree-bears-fruit-after-20-years.html
11. See Further reading.
12. https://en.wikipedia.org/wiki/Olive_Pink_Botanic_Garden
13. http://www.anbg.gov.au/gnp/interns-2002/santalum-acuminatum.html
14. Howes 1948, p. 124

Chapter 4

1. https://archive.is/20130416043642/http://www.worldagroforestrycentre.org/sea/Products/AFDbases/af/asp/SpeciesInfo.asp?SpID=213
2. https://www.sciencedirect.com/topics/neuroscience/theobroma-cacao
3. https://www.feedipedia.org/node/525
4. Paul Vossen: *Olive Oil: History, Production, and Characteristics of the World's Classic Oils* http://hortsci.ashspublications.org/content/42/5/1093.full
5. https://www.researchgate.net/publication/273756549_Tree_Tomato_Tamarillo_potential_Indigenous_alternative_crop_to_Tomato_for_hilly_regions_in_Tamilnadu_India
6. https://www.sciencedirect.com/topics/agricultural-and-biological-sciences/cinnamomum-verum
7. https://www.sciencedirect.com/topics/agricultural-and-biological-sciences/ceratonia-siliqua
8. http://ucavo.ucr.edu/general/historyname.html
9. Mapes, C. and Basurto, F. *Ethnobotany of Mexico: Interactions of People and Plants in Mesoamerica*, 2016, pp. 103–4
10. https://www.researchgate.net/publication/277143748_CURRY_LEAVES_Murraya_koenigii_Linn_Sprengal-_A_MIRCALE_PLANT, in the Indian Journal of Scientific Research 4 (1): 46-52, 2014
11. http://www.ico.org/prices/new-consumption-table.pdf
12. https://www.bbc.co.uk/news/science-environment-46845461
13. https://www.sciencedirect.com/topics/agricultural-and-biological-sciences/prunus-dulcis
14. Information from US National Nutrient Database: https://ndb.nal.usda.gov/ndb/foods/show/12061?fgcd=&manu=&format=Full&count=&max=25&offset=&sort=default&order=asc&qlookup=12061&ds=&q=&qp=&qa=&qn=&q=&ing=
15. Howes 1948, p. 108

Chapter 5

1. https://uses.plantnet-project.org/en/Cordia_subcordata_(PROTA)
2. http://agroforestry.org/images/pdfs/Cordia-kou.pdf
3. http://tropical.theferns.info/viewtropical.php?id=Phoenix+dactylifera
4. His Majesty's Armed Transport.
5. https://news.nationalgeographic.com/news/2013/10/131022-gold-eucalyptus-leaves-mining-geology-science
6. https://blog.csiro.au/national-eucalyptus-day-five-things-you-might-not-know-about-these-flowering-giants/
7. Jackfruit: https://www.ctahr.hawaii.edu/oc/freepubs/pdf/f_n-19.pdf
8. https://web.archive.org/web/20121005003119/http://www.cropsforthefuture.org/publication/Monographs/Jackfruit%20monograph.pdf
9. http://www.florabank.org.au/lucid/key/species%20navigator/media/html/Melaleuca_quinquenervia.htm
10. *The Arabian Nights Entertainments*. Translated by Jonathan Scott, 1811.
11. http://www.tropical.theferns.info/viewtropical.php?id=Cocos+nucifera
12. UN Food and Agriculture Organisation briefing: http://www.fao.org/docrep/x5402e/x5402e11.htm
13. 'Jatropha curcus: A potential biofuel plant for sustainable environmental development.' https://www.sciencedirect.com/science/article/pii/S1364032112000974
14. https://pfaf.org/user/Plant.aspx?LatinName=Shorea+robusta

15. https://www.feedipedia.org/node/54
16. https://www.arganfarm.com/argan-tree-history/

Chapter 6

1. http://www.worldagroforestry.org/treedb/AFTPDFS/Sesbania_sesban.PDF
2. *Lost Crops of Africa*: Volume II, Chapter 14: https://www.nap.edu/read/11763/chapter/16
3. https://keys.lucidcentral.org/keys/v3/eafrinet/weeds/key/weeds/Media/Html/Leucaena_leucocephala_(Leucaena).htm
4. http://www.fao.org/wairdocs/ILRI/x5536E/x5536e0r.htm
5. 'The Lost Crops of the Incas: Little-Known Plants of the Andes with Promise for Worldwide Cultivation.' National Research Council 2005. http://arnoldia.arboretum.harvard.edu/pdf/articles/1990-50-4-lost-crops-of-the-incas.pdf
6. Charles Darwin, from *The Voyage of the Beagle*, published as *Journal and Remarks*, 1839.
7. 'Mangrove forest planted as tsunami shield': https://www.newscientist.com/article/mg22430005-200-mangrove-forest-planted-as-tsunami-shield/
8. http://tropical.theferns.info/viewtropical.php?id=Tamarindus+indica
9. https://fern.org/sites/default/files/news-pdf/Fern%20-%20Return%20of%20the%20Trees.pdf. p.26
10. http://tropical.theferns.info/viewtropical.php?id=Faidherbia+albida
11. Tropical Plants database: Ken Fern. http://www.tropical.theferns.info/viewtropical.php?id=Sclerocarya+birrea

FURTHER READING

Edward Milner, J. *The Tree Book*, Collins and Brown, 1992

Gidmark, D. *The Algonquin Birchbark Canoe*, Shire Ethnography, 1988

Goldstein, M., Simonetti, G. and Watschinger, M. *Complete Guide to Trees and Their Identification*, Macdonald Illustrated, 1984

Howes, F. N. *Nuts: Their Production and Everyday Uses*, Faber and Faber, 1948

Masumoto, D.M. *Epitaph for a Peach*, Harper One, 1995

National Research Council *Lost Crops of Africa Volume III: Fruits*, National Academy Press, 2008

Pakenham, T. *Remarkable Trees of the World*, Weidenfeld and Nicholson, 2002

Plants for a Future *Edible Trees: A Practical and Inspirational Guide from Plants for a Future on how to Grow and Harvest Trees with Edible and Other Useful Produce*, Create Space Independent Publishing, 2013

Russell, T. and Cutler, C. *The World Encyclopaedia of Trees*, Anness Publishing, 2012

Thomas, P. *Trees: Their Natural History*, Cambridge University Press, 2000

Tudge, C. *The Secret Life of Trees*. Penguin Press Science, 2006

Wohlleben, P. *The Hidden Life of Trees*, Collins, 2017

Some worthwhile free downloads

The Natural History Museum: Slavery and the natural world: an invaluable series of book chapters published as PDFs: https://www.nhm.ac.uk/discover/slavery-and-the-natural-world.html

Lost Crops of the Incas: Little Known Plants of the Andes with Promise for Worldwide Cultivation can be downloaded free as a PDF from: https://www.nap.edu/catalog/1398/lost-crops-of-the-incas-little-known-plants-of-the

The Quiet Revolution: How Niger's farmers are re-greening the croplands of the Sahel, is available as a PDF download at: http://www.worldagroforestry.org/downloads/Publications/PDFS/BL17569.pdf

Agroforestry Net, Inc, a non-profit organisation dedicated to providing information about agroforestry, has a website that contains several free downloadable books and factsheets on useful trees from regions across the globe: http://agroforestry.org/FREE-PUBLICATIONS/TRADITIONAL-TREE-PROFILES

PICTURE CREDITS